JANUARY–APRIL

2020

mettle

BIBLE READING NOTES

TO INSPIRE
COURAGE
SPIRIT
CHARACTER

YOUTH FOR CHRIST

CWR

Copyright © YFC and CWR 2019

Published 2020 by CWR, Waverley Abbey House, Waverley Lane, Farnham, Surrey GU9
8EP, England. Registered Charity No. 294387. Registered Limited Company No. 1990308.

 Mettle Bible reading notes are produced in association with British Youth for
Christ. British Youth for Christ is part of Youth for Christ International, a
movement of youth evangelism organisations in over 100 countries of the world.
Please visit yfci.org for the country nearest you.

These notes were previously published in *Mettle* Jan–Apr 2016.

Visit cwr.org.uk/distributors for a list of National Distributors.

Unless otherwise indicated, all Scripture references are from The Holy Bible, New
International Version® Anglicised, NIV® Copyright © 1979, 1984, 2011 by Biblica, Inc.®
Used by permission. All rights reserved worldwide. Other versions used: NLT, New
Living Translation, copyright © 1996, 2004, 2015 by Tyndale House Foundation. Used
by permission of Tyndale House Publishers, Inc., Carol Stream, Illinois 60188. All rights
reserved.

Concept development by YFC and CWR.

Editing, design and production by CWR.

Printed in England by Linney.

CONTENTS

Welcome to

mettle
COURAGE SPIRIT CHARACTER...

Welcome to a new year and a new issue of *Mettle*! Most of us know that the Trinity represents God the Father, Jesus the Son, and the Holy Spirit. But how do they relate to each other, and what should our relationship with Him/Them be like? We'll be finding out.

Then we've got three hot topics. First up: friendships, and why it's great to have friends in the good times as well as in the tough times. Then discipline, which might sound a bit negative, but taking on good habits and getting godly advice is really helpful. Lastly, we'll be looking at how we can use and develop our talents (yes, that includes yours!) to bring glory to God and to help other people.

Our new 'Share' feature lets readers share their thoughts about God, faith and the Bible. If you would like to share anything, feel free to drop us a line at mettle@cwr.org.uk – we'd love to hear from you!

The *Mettle* Team

WED 1 JAN

THE TRINITY

3... 2... 1... Happy New Year!

READ: 1 PETER 1:1–9

KEY VERSE V2
'God the Father... the Spirit... Jesus Christ'

Not only is it a brand-new year, it's a brand-new decade! 2020, here we come! The core topic of this issue of *Mettle* will focus on a famous trio. Can you guess their names? No, not Harry, Ron and Hermione. No, not Alvin, Simon and Theodore. Yes! These being Bible-reading notes, it is, of course, the Father, the Son and the Holy Ghost; otherwise known as the Trinity.

The Trinity sounds a bit odd or mysterious, doesn't it? Like a secret society or one of the factions in the *Divergent* series. Many people find the concept of the Trinity difficult to grasp. But hopefully over these three core sections, we will discover why the Trinity is God's way of connecting with us all the time in exactly the right way.

God the Father, God the Son and God the Holy Spirit are three separate persons who together make up one God. We'll find out more about each of them in these notes, but here's a quick introduction:

- God the Father is our creator, our Father in heaven and the Father of Jesus.
- Jesus, the Father's Son, came to earth as a human to die for our sins and defeat death.
- The Holy Spirit is God living in us. After Jesus returned to heaven, He left His followers the Holy Spirit to help and guide us.

All three were around before the beginning of time, all three were present during the creation of the world and all three will live on forever.

Challenge

Take some time out to write down, in one big list not three separate ones, the different names you already know about for the Father, Jesus and the Spirit (eg creator, Saviour, helper). Then write at the top of your list: 'God'. This may help with understanding the unity and harmony of the Trinity.

Holy moly maths!

READ: MARK 1:9–11

KEY VERSE V10

'he saw heaven being torn open and the Spirit descending on him like a dove.'

As we have said, the Trinity can be weird concept to get your head around. It's a mystery and will remain a mystery to humans this side of heaven. However, there are things about the Trinity we can begin to look into and understand.

The Bible has many examples of this three-person God. Today's passage reveals the Trinity working in perfect harmony. The Son (Jesus) is baptised in the River Jordan. As He comes out of the water, the Holy Spirit descends upon Jesus like a dove. He hears the voice of the Father in heaven saying, 'You are my dearly loved Son, and You bring me great joy.'

How do we explain the Christian doctrine that is the Trinity? How can there be three in one? Another simple example we can use is the mathematical illustration of 1x1x1=1. Here, the value of each independent number is 1 and the value of the multiplied numbers is 1. All are of equal value, but when all are multiplied they still add up to 1. The Trinity makes the Christian faith completely unique. We worship a God who is one and yet three entities. This reveals to us something very key about God – that our God is a God of relationship.

> ## Share
>
> *What are your three favourite pizza toppings?* 'Cheese, chicken and ham.' *What do you think 'the Trinity' means?* 'Three in one.' (Grace, 14)

3 become 1

READ: EPHESIANS 3:14–4:6

KEY VERSE 3:19
'know this love that surpasses knowledge – that you may be filled to the measure of all the fullness of God.'

Back in the 1990s, the Spice Girls topped musical charts with their song '2 become 1'. Though their lyrics take a more secular approach, the point is that in a marriage, two separate people are joined together to make one couple.

Here, in Paul's letter to the Ephesians, we see the wonderful unity and harmony of the Trinity. They are three separate persons but they are still one God – 3 become 1. It is wonderful to see how Paul embraces this Trinity God in his prayer to the Ephesians. This great and mighty God is so awesome that Paul can do nothing more than kneel in worship before Him. He prays that the Ephesians may be strengthened by the Spirit; that the Spirit may give them the power to live for God every day and to be a disciple and follower of Christ. Finally, Paul prays that Christ may dwell deeply in their hearts.

Paul wants us to understand this amazing love of God in its immeasurable dimensions: its width, its depth, its length and its height. This love for mankind is just awesome! The Trinity is a living, vibrant relationship and we can be caught up in it as we live to serve a living, dynamic Almighty God.

66 *Share*

What is your favourite trilogy (books or films)? *'Star Wars.'*
What do you think 'the Trinity' means? *'The connection between the three entities of God.'* (Daniel, 15)

CORE THEME | THE TRINITY 1

Weekend

4/5 JAN

In a nutshell

READ: JOHN 3:16

KEY VERSE V16

'For God so loved the world that he gave his one and only Son'

In 2009, Tim Tebow, an American football player, was competing in a televised championship football game. Before the match, he felt led to write John 3:16 under his eyes for all the world to see while he played. After his team won the match, 94 million people googled John 3:16.

Our reading, John 3:16, is probably one of the most well-known Bible verses and that's because it is so fundamental to what Christians believe. Sometimes referred to as the 'gospel in a nutshell', it's a great summary of the central message of Christianity.

In this one verse, we see a God who loves. He loves the world so much that He gave Himself, in the form of Jesus, His one and only Son, so that we can receive eternal life. Not only is God longing for a relationship with us – He's also a God who is relationship. He is in relationship with Himself as the Trinity.

Because Adam and Eve disobeyed God and ate the forbidden apple in the Garden of Eden, sin entered into the human race, causing a great divide between us and God. But God's longing for relationship with us inspired His rescue plan. His Son would bear the weight of the whole world's sin and pay the price for it on the cross. It is only through Jesus' death that we are brought into a right relationship with the Father, and receive the Holy Spirit to live in us. We no longer look forward to an eternity without God, but look forward to living with Him forever. What a fantastic gift!

Pray

Thank You, Father, for giving Your one and only Son to die on the cross so that, through Him, we may enjoy relationship with You on earth now, and look forward to an eternity shared with You. Amen.

Secret agent

READ: HAGGAI 2:1–9

KEY VERSE V5
'my Spirit remains among you. Do not fear.'

In the Old Testament, before Jesus' life, death and resurrection, the Holy Spirit acted like an agent of God. (A bit like James Bond but without the guns, cars, women... actually nothing like James Bond.) The Holy Spirit empowered specific people at a specific time to do God's will. Here in today's reading, we read a promise that the Spirit will remain with the nation of Israel – He will not just be with one or two people – and He will never leave.

Haggai records the Israelites' return home from exile; their former cities are in ruin, their culture erased and their religion forgotten. As they begin to rebuild their nation, God promises that He'll remain with them just as He did when they crossed the Red Sea hundreds of years before, seeking the Promised Land.

From the very early days of Abraham and Isaac, God had chosen these people to represent Him to other nations. They often got it wrong and turned away from His rules for life, but God continued to remain with them by His Spirit. When we turn our backs on God, it is His Holy Spirit who remains with us and draws us back into relationship with Him.

66 *Share*

What are your three favourite pizza toppings? *'BBQ meatballs, BBQ chicken and BBQ sauce.'* ***What do you think 'the Trinity' means?*** *'Father, Son and Holy Spirit.'* (Cam, 15)

Love with all you've got

READ: DEUTERONOMY 6:1–19

KEY VERSE V4
'the LORD our God, the LORD is one.'

Imagine a world without YouTube... what else would we watch?! It's an amazing platform for anyone and everyone to communicate whatever they want to with the wider world. It's easy to spend a lot of time watching video after video after video... from debates about Brexit, to cat fails. Unfortunately, God doesn't vlog – but He does love to hear from us.

In today's passage we see Moses, towards the end of his life, preaching to the people of Israel before they enter the Promised Land. Moses wants these former slaves of Egypt to understand who their God is. The words of our key verse today are the words of the Jewish Shema, recited by devout Jews twice a day to ensure that they remember how different their God is from other gods.

Today we read that God is a 'jealous God' (v15), which means we can't love Him and love other 'gods' at the same time. These 'gods' may be social media, football, fashion or money. Whatever we're spending most of our time, energy and affection on, that's our god. So let's respond to God's amazing, huge love for us with the love He deserves: 'Love the LORD your God with all your heart and with all your soul and with all your strength' (v5).

CORE THEME | THE TRINITY 1

Share

When you pray, do you pray to God, Jesus or the Holy Spirit?
'I pray mostly to Jesus because He's my go-to.' (Jacob, 16)

Pray 1-on-1

☰ READ: MATTHEW 6:7–13

KEY VERSE V8
*'for your Father knows what you need before you
ask him.'*

How do you maintain your closest friendships? Most of us
love, communicate, trust, and spend time with our nearest
and dearest. All these are important in keeping our earthly
friendships together, but what about our relationship with
our heavenly Father?

Already we know that God is a God of relationship – not
just within the Trinity, but also with us. So we need to be
communicating with Him to keep maintaining and growing
this amazing relationship with the Trinity.

Knowing that He would not be with His disciples for long,
Jesus teaches them how to pray.

- First, He says, go into your room and close the door. God
  has a relationship with you individually. Of course, there
  are times of group prayers in church or with friends, but
  prayer should also be lots of one-to-one time with God.
- Second, don't use fancy words for the sake of it, but
  speak honestly from the heart.
- And thirdly, Jesus tells us that God knows what we need
  before we even ask!

So let's talk to Him, knowing that He cares about every
aspect of our lives.

Share

When you pray, do you pray to God, Jesus or the Holy Spirit?
*'I pray mostly to God because that's what I'm used to and
from the Lord's Prayer, "Our Father..."'* (Ethan, 17)

CORE THEME | THE TRINITY 1

Who's that man?

READ: GENESIS 32:22–32

KEY VERSE V24
*'So Jacob was left alone, and a man wrestled with him
till daybreak.'*

Do you know the meaning of your name? Do you think
your parents chose your name because of its meaning or
because they liked the sound of it? During Bible times the
choice of a name was very important – it defined your
character and temperament.

Jacob means 'deceiver' and, even before he was
born, Jacob wrestled with his elder twin for his future
inheritance. He then goes on to deceive his own father and,
in turn, is later deceived by his own father-in-law. Then
what happens? Well, further on in his life, when Jacob
takes his whole family away from his crafty father-in-law,
Jacob has a very interesting wrestling match one night
with a man – or was He just a man?

What man can bless unless that man is God? What man
changes a person's name and identity (Jacob to Israel)
unless that man is God? If Jesus is God in bodily form
(Col. 2:9), then when God appeared to people during the
Old Testament, this was as one member of the Holy Trinity.
These mysterious appearances often hint at this member
possibly being Jesus – not yet come to earth.

Pray
*Thank You, Jesus, that You are involved in the lives of Your
people. Thank You that before You were born in Bethlehem,
You made Yourself known to key characters at key times to
help Your nation of Israel grow. Amen.*

CORE THEME | THE TRINITY 1

Look up, Look ahead

READ: GENESIS 18:1–20

KEY VERSE V2
'Abraham looked up and saw three men standing nearby.'

What does 2020 look like for you? Maybe you have exams to take, subjects to choose or colleges or universities to visit. Maybe you have an exciting trip planned or role in a major production. The future might look exciting but it can also look daunting.

Abraham was not feeling positive about his future. He and his wife, Sarah, had no children to care for them in their old age. But then one day, he looked up...

We have seen how Jesus appeared in bodily form (often in the guise of an angel or messenger) to individuals in the Old Testament. This time, God appears to Abraham as one of three men. The Bible is quite specific in the number of men who appeared; Abraham even asked Sarah for three bowls to feed them (v6). But the Bible also tells us several times that it was the Lord who spoke (vv13,17,20).

The Lord spoke and prophesied about the future birth of Isaac (v10), but the description is of three men. Did the Lord appear together with two angels? Whatever happened, we can be sure that the Trinity was present in the world and at work before the birth of Isaac and the creation of the nation of Israel. He was and always is there for us – so let's look up.

CORE THEME | THE TRINITY 1

Share

When you pray, do you pray to God, Jesus or the Holy Spirit?
'I pray to God because He is all three, so all are included.'
(Josh, 16)

FRIENDSHIP

With a little help from my friends

READ: JOHN 15:1–17

KEY VERSE V15
'Instead, I have called you friends, for everything that I learned from my Father I have made known to you.'

All the best TV shows have an amazing friendship at the heart of the story: Joey and Chandler; Sherlock Holmes and Dr Watson; Leslie Knope and Ann Perkins. They might have their ups and downs, but they are always there for each other.

As we begin to look at the topic of friendship, think about the people you would call your friends. What are they like? Are you alike or are you completely different? What made you want to be their friend in the first place? What memories do you share?

Relationships with friends can be some of the most rewarding relationships in your life. You may lose touch with some friends, but others may never leave you. And memories and experiences of these friendships in our younger years will help us to forge new ones when we're adults.

Of course, friendship is not all a walk in the park! Sometimes friendships go wrong. A friendship can go through difficult times as well as rewarding times. Jesus' disciples would certainly agree with this. Jesus chose 12 young men to be His closest friends, to share all that He was with them: His heart, His life, His love and His sorrow. In true friendship we share all aspects of our lives, which leaves us open and vulnerable to the other person. This may be one reason why some of us find it hard to forge deep friendships.

During our time looking at friendships, we'll seek to understand: what makes a friendship either good or bad, what to do when friendship goes wrong, how to be a good friend and what it means to be friends with God.

Pray

Lord God, thank You for Your friendship and love for me. Help me to see what good friendship is and to appreciate it with a thankful heart. Amen.

Be careful of the company you keep

READ: PROVERBS 17:14–22

KEY VERSE V17
'A friend loves at all times, and a brother is born for a time of adversity.'

In the film, *Mean Girls**, Cady is a 16-year-old who starts high school after years of living in the jungle and being home-schooled by her parents. She soon makes friends with Damian and Janis but they are not part of the 'cool crowd'. The popular girls are called 'the plastics' and they look perfect, wear designer clothes, have expensive cars – but are really mean. When the plastics take an interest in Cady, Cady ends up spending a lot of time with them and becomes like them. Not only does she start dressing like them, she becomes mean as well. After much drama, revenge and back-stabbing (the plot's a bit complicated – you might need to watch the film), Cady realises that her real friends are Damian and Janis who like her for who she is and not for what she is wearing.

The plastics were not true friends. They were only happy to be seen with others who looked good or wore fashionable clothes. There might be groups of girls or boys that you know who are only concerned about image and popularity and not about being kind. A true friend is one who sticks with you, no matter what the circumstances: his or her love is not dependent on things going well.

HOT TOPIC | FRIENDSHIP 1

➕ *Challenge*

Take an honest look at what type of friend you are. Are you willing to stick by people no matter what? Or do you distance yourself when a friend is struggling?

*Mean Girls, Paramount Pictures, 2004

Outfit choices

≡ **READ: COLOSSIANS 3:7–12**

KEY VERSE V12
'clothe yourselves with compassion, kindness, humility, gentleness and patience.'

➡ How are you dressed today? Here's a quick checklist: top [√], trousers [√], jacket [√], socks [√], pants [√], patience [?], humility [?]. Most of us like to make sure that we are dressed appropriately for the weather or what we might be doing, but do we make an effort to put on attributes that we might need for the day ahead?

Our character says something about us. It tells those around us what type of person we are. When we first meet people, we usually see a glimpse of their character; if positive, we might think to ourselves, *I like them*, and a friendship is born. Most of us would want to be a friend of someone who showed the qualities mentioned in today's reading because we could have confidence in them and would be able to trust them.

What's more important, though, is whether we want to be the type of friend who shows these qualities ourselves. The Bible tells us to clothe ourselves with kindness, humility etc. Why? Well, in the same way that others see our clothing, God wants these qualities to be evident in our lives so that others can see them. As we allow the Holy Spirit to work in us, we'll become more like Jesus – and these qualities will grow in us.

➕ *Challenge*

Try writing down a list of words that describe your character. When your friends spend time with you, what qualities do they see in you?

HOT TOPIC | FRIENDSHIP 1

Bear with...

READ: COLOSSIANS 3:13–17

KEY VERSE V13
'Bear with each other and forgive one another if any of you has a grievance against someone.'

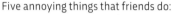

Five annoying things that friends do:
1. You did something embarrassing years ago and they still find it hilarious to talk about it.
2. They tease you and make knowing looks when someone you like walks by.
3. They talk all the way through your favourite movie – or worse, tell you what happens at the end!
4. They order a salad and then eat your chips!
5. They 'borrow' your clothes and never return them.

Our friends may have different qualities from us, which at times may be frustrating but doesn't necessarily make them a bad person.

We all have our faults. And, sometimes, something we see as a fault in someone else might not be a fault at all – just something we don't like! Our priorities may not be the same as another's, and we could easily mistake this for a fault or a flaw in their character. Friendship, however, means having the grace to allow them to be unique and to forgive any genuine faults they show. After all, we have our own faults, as well as our strange little habits!

Think

Do any of your friends wind you up? Is this because of a genuine fault in them? If so, perhaps it's time to forgive them. If it's just because of a strange habit, ask God for grace to tolerate it!

HOT TOPIC | FRIENDSHIP 1

19

Friends to carry us

READ: 1 SAMUEL 18:1–3; 19:1–7

KEY VERSE 18:3
'And Jonathan made a covenant with David because he loved him as himself.'

In Tolkien's the book, *The Lord of the Rings: The Return of the King*, Frodo is physically and mentally exhausted from having had to carry the ring. Sam can't carry it for him, so instead carries Frodo the rest of the way to Mordor. Sam did what he could to help his best friend.

David and Jonathan are another example of a deep and solid friendship that we find in the Old Testament. They protected and loved each other in all they did. In the NIV translation of our reading today it says that they were even 'one in spirit' (18:1). The hallmarks of their relationship were closeness and trust.

Saul was king and Jonathan was the king's son. When David was in danger as a consequence of Saul's jealousy and fear, Jonathan warned David and even went so far as to plead his case to his father. Putting his friendship above the king's orders could have cost Jonathan his life at times. But Jonathan's actions meant that David survived and went on to be one of the greatest kings ever, leading Israel into a period of prosperity and wholehearted worship of God.

Pray

Dear Lord Jesus, You once said, 'There is no greater love than to lay down one's life for one's friends.' You laid down Your life for me so that I might have a relationship with God the Father. Thank You. Please show me how to be a true and good friend, like Jonathan was and You are. Amen.

HOT TOPIC | FRIENDSHIP 1

Selfless friend

READ: 1 SAMUEL 26:1–25

KEY VERSE V6
'"I'll go with you," said Abishai.'

King Saul's jealousy of David had got the better of him once again and he got his army together to seek David out and kill him. David knew where they were camping overnight and made a plan to show the king that he meant him no harm. David was to enter the enemy camp in the dead of night and take something from close to the king. This was to show him that he could have killed him but chose not to. (David knew that Saul was God's anointed king and he would not remove Saul from the throne without God's say-so.) This mission was going to be dangerous and David asked two of his closest allies to go with him. Abishai agreed. He risked his own life for David.

Of course, we will probably never have to risk our lives for anyone, but there are times when our friends need us to go out of our way to help them. For example, they may need someone to talk to on the same night that we've been invited to a party. Or a friend may need encouragement and cheering up because others have been unkind and thoughtless. Sometimes, helping might make us vulnerable to ridicule and attack as well. But this is an important part of what being a true friend is – putting others before ourselves.

HOT TOPIC | FRIENDSHIP 1

Think

What sacrifices have you made in the past to help out a friend? Would you be prepared to stand up for your friends even if it meant that you could suffer too?

Weekend

18/19 JAN

It's good to talk

READ: ROMANS 5:1–11

KEY VERSE V11
'we also boast in God through our Lord Jesus Christ, through whom we have now received reconciliation.'

How often do you talk to your best friend? Once a year? Once a month? It won't be a very close friendship unless you talk to them more frequently than that. If they really are your best friend, you will want to hear about what they have been doing and how they are.

Jesus offers us friendship – not just with God the Son but also God the Father and God the Holy Spirit. We've been given the opportunity to have a wonderful relationship with the Almighty God. So how does this work? Our Scripture reading today tells us how Jesus came and died for us, even though we were still sinners. It is because of Jesus' death that we have been made right in the sight of God. Now our friendship with God can be restored.

It doesn't end there. Our reading also tells us that because God loves us so dearly, He has given us the Holy Spirit to fill our hearts with His love (v5). We don't deserve any of this, but God wanted to reach out to us and provide a way for us to be His friends. Jesus the Son takes away our sins when we confess them and say sorry, the Father hears our prayers because of what Jesus has done and the Spirit guides us and helps us to live godly lives. God provides a friendship that helps us in everything we do.

However, friendship with God can be like any other friendship. The more you talk and listen to what each other has to say, the deeper the relationship can go. When we don't talk and listen to God so much we can lose touch with Him. So stay connected and keep talking.

 ## Challenge

Try asking yourself a few questions to gauge where you are with God: how deep is my friendship with God? How much time do I spend getting to know God more and listening to Him? How can I deepen my friendship with God?

Take a step of faith

READ: JAMES 2:14–24

KEY VERSE V23

'"Abraham believed God, and it was credited to him as righteousness," and he was called God's friend.'

Have you ever played a game where one person is blindfolded and another person is giving directions about which way to go? You have to be able to trust that the person is guiding you the right way.

Abraham had a strong faith and deep confidence in God because he knew God to be his great, good and faithful friend. He trusted God's words to him and chose to listen and follow what God said. Taking God at His word, Abraham stepped out from all that he knew and loved and followed God into a strange land with an uncertain destination. Later on, he was willing to surrender the most precious thing he had into God's hands. What faith! What friendship! What a challenge! If it came to it, could you trust God with everything you have?

We are told that God saw Abraham as godly and righteous, because of his faith. Perhaps, to us, Abraham is an extraordinary character with the kind of faith we could never have. Or maybe Abraham was just like you and me; a person who tried to hear God, do his best to follow Him and rely on Him to guide his path through life. We don't have to be extraordinary to be God's friend. We make a start by choosing to trust Him.

Pray

Thank You, Father, that You are a true and trustworthy friend. Help me to put my confidence in You and to look to You for guidance in my life. Amen.

HOT TOPIC | FRIENDSHIP 1

Everyone's invited!

READ: LUKE 5:27–32

KEY VERSE V29
'Levi held a great banquet for Jesus... and a large crowd of tax collectors and others were eating with them.'

If you were going out for a meal, who would you take with you? Or, if you won a holiday abroad, who would be the best person to take? Would it be someone you didn't know very well or your best friend? Probably your friend! Most of us wouldn't choose people we know very little about or people who are seen as undesirable by others. In Jesus' time, tax collectors were despised. They were usually dishonest, untrustworthy, greedy and corrupt. Worst of all, they took money from their own people and gave it to the Romans, who had invaded the country. Tax collectors were traitors but Jesus wanted to spend time with them.

Jesus chose outsiders, like tax collectors, because He wanted to bring the good news to those who really needed it, not the people who thought they already knew it all. Jesus wasn't afraid to be seen with those no one else wanted to be seen with! He put His own reputation at risk so that they might know God.

It's easy to stick with friends or people like ourselves but a little bit more challenging to be friendly with those who seem so different. Jesus wasn't in some exclusive clique, He invites everyone to the party! Let's follow His example.

HOT TOPIC | FRIENDSHIP 1

Think

Think about this: who do you try to avoid? Who are the people you just don't get along with? Do they know God? Could you be the person who shares God's love with them?

It takes two

READ: ECCLESIASTES 4:7–12

KEY VERSE V9
'Two are better than one'

Starsky and Hutch, Morse and Lewis, Holmes and Watson, Scott and Bailey, Peralta and Santiago. Have you noticed how many police and detective dramas have two people as the main characters? It seems that if one gets in trouble, the other is on hand to help them out. Being in a duo also means that they have someone to discuss the case with, argue about who is the murderer, tell jokes to and eat endless doughnuts with. It would make pretty poor TV if we watched them do all this on their own.

In today's passage, Solomon is having one of his thoughtful days. He's looking around and wondering about the meaning of life. (Not exactly the life and soul of the party!) He spies a man working on his own, and reflects how much better it is when we have a friend to do life with.

You might understand the value of teamwork and enjoy it when necessary but actually prefer to do things on your own. Nevertheless, it's always good to have a friend around; someone you can talk to, laugh with and help out. I'm sure we can all remember times when having someone else with us would have made a real difference to a situation we were facing.

Challenge

If you don't already have someone to mentor you, why not try to find someone? This might be a youth leader or any older Christian you trust. It can make a big difference in your life and your faith!

HOT TOPIC | FRIENDSHIP 1

Happy families?

READ: EPHESIANS 6:1–4

KEY VERSE V2
'"Honour your father and mother" – which is the first commandment with a promise'

Maybe you have a very close loving relationship with your parents or carers, and that's great. However, many people struggle to get on with their nearest and dearest. For TV examples of extreme family dysfunction, there's plenty of choice, whether for comedy or for drama – probably because it's a subject many of us can relate to!

Most parents want the best for their children and are able to pass on helpful advice from their own past experience: be polite, work hard, always take a jacket with you and don't over-pluck your eyebrows! However, we need to remember that parents are people who make mistakes too. If they are asking you to do something wrong, then it isn't always right to obey them.*

God's ideal is that we grow up in a loving, supportive family atmosphere. Sometimes, that isn't the reality but if you do have loving parents or carers, listen to what they say because they usually know what they are talking about.

 Pray
Ask God to help you when you struggle with doing as your parents ask. And if you are really struggling at home, talk to someone you trust. Ask God to bring peace in your home and friendship between you and your mum, dad or carer.

*If you are being pressured to do something that you know is wrong, talk to an adult you trust or contact ChildLine.

HOT TOPIC | FRIENDSHIP 1

FRI 24 JAN

Your church needs YOU

READ: ROMANS 12:1–13

KEY VERSE V5
'in Christ we, though many, form one body, and each member belongs to all the others.'

What's your church like? Is it made up of perfect people who always look beautiful and never get anything wrong? Probably not – but if it is then that sounds quite scary!

Your church family is not much different to the family you live with. There are going to be times when personalities clash, people might disagree and may even fall out occasionally. It would be great if churches were perfect, but unfortunately that's not the case. The Church is made up of real people and people aren't perfect.

Worshipping God together as the body of Christ also includes loving one another. As our key verse says, we are many parts of one body, and we all belong to each other. Belonging to each other and to the body of Christ can be difficult, but when we love one another it is the best place to be. Within the Church family, we can use our gifts and see others using the gifts God has given them. We try to work in harmony with each other and to build friendships that enable us to grow as Christians. If each of us is not doing our part, then the Church is not flourishing as God intended. Your local church needs you – yes, you! Your friendship might be just what someone needs. It could be the start of something amazing for you too.

 Think

How meaningful are your friendships with people at church? How can you get to know them better? How can you serve them?

HOT TOPIC | FRIENDSHIP 1

**WEEKEND
25/26 JAN**

DISCIPLINE

Get the good habits

READ: JAMES 2:14–26

KEY VERSE V14
'What good is it... if someone claims to
have faith but has no deeds?'

What bad habits annoy you most? Maybe your
dad has a really loud and embarrassing laugh, the
person who sits near you at lunch eats really loudly,
or your friend just can't help butting in when you're
speaking. Do you have any habits that you know
annoy other people? Have you perhaps tried to
break your bad habit?

We all have habits. Some of them are good, some
are bad, and some are just plain weird! Think about
your routines in the morning or evening, either
when getting up or going to bed. Do you do things
in a certain order or way each day? For example,

some people can't have breakfast until they're dressed and ready in the morning. Others have to eat breakfast just to have the energy to get dressed and ready!

Lots of people have written or spoken about how long it takes to make something a habit, with varying lengths of time suggested – it's not one size fits all. It takes time, effort and commitment to turn something into a habit. We can think of developing habits as developing certain disciplines (or practices). As Christians, it's really important to think about what disciplines we want to develop, so that we can make a start on them. Having faith in Jesus is great and really important, but sooner or later this faith should affect our words and our actions, which can become signs of our faith. Over the next few days we'll be thinking about some of the ways in which we can aim for our actions and words to change – spiritual disciplines we can develop to live in a wiser, more godly way.

Pray

Lord God, as I think about spiritual disciplines, please show me which habits I should work on and develop. Help me to grow in my faith and to follow You more closely. Amen.

A breath of fresh air

READ: 2 TIMOTHY 3:10–17

KEY VERSE V16
*'All Scripture is God-breathed and is useful for
teaching, rebuking, correcting and training in
righteousness'*

The first discipline we're looking at is Bible study. The
very fact you are reading this shows that you're probably
prepared to develop this discipline!

Today's verse points out why this habit is important.
The Bible is a very important way in which God guides us.
By studying it, we are allowing God to equip us to become
better followers of Him and to fulfil the plans He has for us.

If you don't yet study the Bible every day, challenge
yourself to set aside 15–20 minutes to do this and reflect
on what you've read (as you've done today!). Commit
to doing this every day and you'll be on the journey to
making it a habit. Think about the time of day when you
read the Bible. Are you always in a rush in the morning,
struggling to fit it in? Do you find it difficult to stay awake
and concentrate just before bed? Figure out when the best
time is for you.

If you have already developed the discipline of studying
God's Word at a regular point in the day, then think about
how you could bring it in at other times as well. For
example, maybe you could stick a Bible verse onto your
mirror where you will see it often, or set one as a reminder
on your phone. Try to make God's Word a more central
part of your life.

HOT TOPIC | DISCIPLINE 1

➕ Challenge

*Reflect again on what you've read today. What might be
an appropriate challenge for you in the coming week?*

Can we have a chat?

☰ READ: 1 THESSALONIANS 5:16–24

KEY VERSE V17
'pray continually'

→ Another key discipline we need to focus on is prayer. There are many different reasons as to why prayer is important, and today's verse makes it clear that prayer is crucial and should be a central part of our daily life.

When something significant happens during the day, is your first thought to turn to God in prayer? It may be to ask for help or it may be to thank Him for something. So many people don't think to pray about something until much later on. The initial reaction might instead be something like: how can I deal with the situation myself? Or: who can I message about the situation?

As well as prayer being a feature throughout our day, we should also set aside specific time each day to devote to prayer. The issue is that our minds often wander. We start off praying and end up thinking about what snacks there are in the house. There are lots of different methods you can use to become more focused as you pray. Some people find that journaling really helps them process things and keep a record of what they've been praying about for future use.

 ## *Challenge*
Start writing your prayers down in a journal or on your phone, as if you're writing to God. Every so often, look back over past prayers and praise God for all He's done.

Stick together

READ: HEBREWS 10:19–25

KEY VERSE V25
'not giving up meeting together, as some are in the habit of doing, but encouraging one another'

In today's world, we often have many different opportunities open to us and so our lives can be very busy. With school or college work, sports clubs, socialising with friends, part-time jobs and loads of other things that take up our time, it can be a challenge to fit in any involvement with our local church and/or youth group. Attending church and meeting with other Christians can easily slip down our list of priorities. But today's reading reminds us that meeting with other Christians is another important discipline to develop.

When we meet with other Christians, we should be in the habit of encouraging one another and spurring each other on in our faith. It's not easy to follow Jesus – we need each other's backing. Think about who you generally turn to for advice when you need help in making a decision. Do they usually give godly advice? Think too about what happens when people come to you for advice. Do you tell them what you think they want to hear, or do you really think and pray about the advice you give? Proverbs 27:17 tells us that, as friends, we can be instrumental in developing each other. Do you take that seriously in your own relationships?

HOT TOPIC | DISCIPLINE 1

Think

Do you allow other Christians to influence your life by meeting with them regularly? What relationships might God be encouraging you to invest more time in?

33

Work it out

 READ: COLOSSIANS 3:16–25

KEY VERSE V23
*'Whatever you do, work at it with all your heart,
as working for the Lord, not for human masters'*

HOT TOPIC | DISCIPLINE 1

⟶ Yesterday we thought about how being involved in our local church and spending time with other Christians are important habits to develop. The way in which we serve and give our time and skills for others is another important spiritual discipline. You may already be heavily involved in your church, maybe helping with the children's work, serving tea and coffee, or playing in the worship band. Today's verse tells us that everything we do (not just volunteering at church) should be done as if we are doing it for God.

Perhaps helping at church on a Sunday is already a priority for you. But how about at other times in the week? Are there other opportunities during the week when you could use your time to serve God? Could you offer to babysit so that someone can attend an event at church? Or could you perhaps visit a member of the church who is elderly or unwell?

We're reminded by our verse today that even when we're not obviously serving God in what we're doing, we should do whatever we do as if it were for God – that even includes things like getting your homework in on time and doing the washing up! Let's see all of it as honouring God.

 Pray
Father, thank You for giving me skills and talents. Please show me how to use them and let me see every opportunity I have as an opportunity to serve You. Amen.

All for one

READ: 1 CHRONICLES 16:23–36

KEY VERSE V29
'Worship the LORD in the splendour of his holiness.'

The next spiritual discipline we are going to look at is worship. Worship isn't just about listening to all the latest Christian song – in fact, worship features throughout the Bible. In Genesis we read of how Cain and Abel made offerings to God (Gen. 4:3–5). We can read and enjoy David's songs of worship in the book of Psalms, and also read about him dancing before the LORD (2 Sam. 6:14). We can even find amazing descriptions of worship in Revelation (eg Rev. 19:1–8). And right throughout the Bible there are numerous other examples of people worshipping God.

To worship means to acknowledge how great God is, with both our words and our actions. Worship should not be all about us but should focus on God. Taking part in worship reminds us of, and focuses us on, who God is and who we are: people created and loved by God.

Because of the many different ways that worship is given to God in the Bible, we can be reminded that there is no one right way to do it – a guitar isn't a necessity. Worship isn't just about singing songs at church on a Sunday or at a big event, as good as that is. Our whole lives should be acts of worship (Rom. 12:1), pointing to God and who He is.

Think

Reflect on your own experiences of worship. Do you think that worship is a regular part of your life, or is it mostly saved for Sundays?

HOT TOPIC | DISCIPLINE 1

Weekend

No train, no gain

READ: 1 CORINTHIANS 9:24–27

KEY VERSE V25
'Everyone who competes in the games goes into strict training.'

Over the weekend we will take a quick break from looking at individual disciplines we should be trying to develop and think more generally about why being disciplined is important.

Some people seem to be remarkably self-disciplined. They manage to complete all their homework on the night they get it, and never leave deadlines hanging over them until the last minute. The rest of us might need to pull the occasional all-nighter!

Paul gives us real food for thought in today's reading. He uses metaphors to explain the need to be disciplined in training ourselves to do what God wants us to do; in living well so that we can impact well. If we profess to be Christians and follow Christ, then we need to practise what we preach.

Many people are put off Christianity because they see the hypocrisy with which so many so-called 'Christians' live their lives. On the one hand, these 'Christians' talk about a message of peace and forgiveness, but then they gossip nastily about other people. Or perhaps they believe that everybody should attend all the church services and youth events on offer, but then they go out and get drunk every Friday night.

Paul likens this kind of behaviour to the risk of being disqualified. What good is it to say that people should live a Christian lifestyle, if we are not seen to make the effort ourselves? When we are seen to live up to the claims we make, then people will respect us and be more interested in what we have to say.

 ## Challenge

Do you need to develop more self-discipline and train yourself further in any aspects of your life? Ask God to coach you in your training.

Tell the world

≡ **READ: ACTS 1:1–11**

KEY VERSE V8

'you will be my witnesses... to the ends of the earth.'

We're back again to looking at some of the spiritual disciplines that are great for us to develop in. Next up, evangelism. If you find the concept of sharing your faith scary and uncomfortable, you are not alone. But if we truly believe the good news of the gospel, if we catch a glimpse of Jesus and see how amazing He is, if we care for the people around us in a similar way to how He does, surely we will be inspired to share Him with those people.

Notice how today's key verse uses the word 'will'. Evangelism is a command, not an option. Of course, it's as we're filled with the Holy Spirit that evangelism becomes easier and more natural. But, even so, we're called to choose to take the opportunities to share our faith when those opportunities arrive – not try to ignore them. We're also called to pray for more of these opportunities.

As followers of Jesus, we've been told to get on with the job of telling and showing others who He is and what He has done for them. We'll get mixed reactions, that's for sure, but there may be some who listen and turn to Jesus – and that makes it worth it.

🔾 *Think*

Many people who become Christians hear about Jesus through a friend. Do you pray for your friends, asking God that they would come to know Him? Do you look for opportunities to talk to them about God?

HOT TOPIC | DISCIPLINE 1

Treasure

READ: 1 CORINTHIANS 16:1–4

KEY VERSE V2
'each one of you should set aside a sum of money in keeping with your income'

Today's spiritual discipline is about how we use our money. Money can be quite an awkward topic of conversation, but throughout the Bible there are a lot of references to money: how we are to use it and how we are to give some to the work of God. As young people, it can be easy to think that this doesn't really apply to us. However, as we think about the need to form positive habits, it makes sense to start young – even if all we have is a little bit of change.

The Bible frequently warns of the dangers of becoming too attached to money and riches. Luke 12:34 says, 'For where your treasure is, there your heart will be also.' If we are prepared to give money for God's purposes, then it communicates that He's a priority for us.

Proverbs 3:5 tells us to 'Trust in the LORD with all your heart and lean not on your own understanding'. Are we prepared to put our trust in God's ability to provide for us? Do we perhaps think we'll be better off if we can buy a new device or the latest trainers, or follow the latest fashion trend? Or do we sacrifice our money to God, putting Him first and trusting that He will look after our every need?

HOT TOPIC | DISCIPLINE 1

Pray
Thank You, God, that You were willing to sacrifice Your Son for me. I want to put You first. Please show me where to spend less money so that I can give more to You and Your work. Amen.

Give it up

READ: MATTHEW 6:16–18

KEY VERSE V16
'When you fast'

→ The last spiritual discipline we'll look at is fasting. Many of us may find fasting the spiritual discipline we struggle with the most. But our reading talks about *when* you fast, not *if* you fast.

What's the point in fasting, though? Life can get ridiculously busy, and sometimes things just get in the way of our relationship with God. Going without something gives us extra time to spend with God and reminds us to turn to Him in prayer instead. It also helps us to depend on God and gain a clearer spiritual perspective on life.

So how do you do it? Traditionally, fasting has involved going without a meal in order to focus and rely more on God. But there are also other forms of fasting: ditching your phone, turning off the TV, not listening to music, going without just one kind of food, only drinking water etc.

If you've never fasted before, it's best to start small and be realistic. If you're intending to fast from food, talk to a parent about it, make sure it's safe for you to do so and you're doing it for the right reason, and try missing just one meal. Remember that fasting isn't meant to bog you down, it's meant to get you closer to God, experiencing more of life to the full!

 Challenge

Have you ever fasted from something? Why or why not? How could you develop this as one of your spiritual disciplines?

HOT TOPIC | DISCIPLINE 1

Live your life

READ: ECCLESIASTES 8:9–17

KEY VERSE V15
'So I commend the enjoyment of life, because there is nothing better for a person'

Often we think of disciplined people as boring, never able to have fun or be spontaneous. Many people believe that the Christian life has to be like that. But that's just not the case! In today's verse we are told that it is good to enjoy life and have fun. It sounds silly, but that's not something we often think about as being important as Christians.

We don't need to cut ourselves off from the people around us, thinking that's what a good follower of Jesus should do. That's not what God wants at all. We're told to get out there and have a great time!

It's good to go out with our friends and create great memories with them. But we also need to be wise. Being a self-disciplined Christian means that we can have fun as long as we remain in control of our actions and words, and know where to draw the line. There's a difference between a) going to a party and dancing, talking, laughing and having a great time, and b) going to a party, getting drunk and making bad decisions that we'll regret. It's important to have boundaries in place, even if our friends don't, so that the fun stays fun.

HOT TOPIC | DISCIPLINE 1

Think

How do you relate to those around you who aren't Christians? Are you able to show self-discipline in the way you conduct yourself? How might God want you to change the way you act around others?

Keep it up

 READ: DEUTERONOMY 6:20–25

KEY VERSE V24
*'The Lord commanded us to obey all these decrees…
so that we might always prosper'*

Developing spiritual disciplines is rather like an athlete training for an event. Athletes think about all aspects of their lifestyle. As well as physical exercise, they take care to eat the right food, and they avoid drugs and alcohol. In training ourselves to be godly, we need to think about all aspects of our lives, and we need to do this consistently. It is no use focusing on just one of the spiritual disciplines. All have a significant part to play in helping us get closer to God and become more like Jesus.

We may think that we are doing pretty well with our spiritual disciplines, but let's be challenged by the way that athletes don't get complacent and stop working hard. They may be the best and always come first, but they strive to be even better. There's always something more that could be achieved; another record that could be broken.

Today's reading reminds us that we don't follow God's commands and develop spiritual disciplines just to feel good about ourselves. No, the reward is much greater than that. If we follow God's commands, we open ourselves up to receive all kinds of blessings. What an incentive. Better than any Olympic gold medal!

 Pray

Lord, please show me the ways in which You would like me to develop. Give me the strength and the self-discipline to become more of the person You want me to be. Amen.

01

TALENT

#gifted
READ: EPHESIANS 4:7–13

KEY VERSE V8
'[Christ] gave gifts to his people.'

Congratulations! You're talented! You might already know that. Maybe you have a good idea what your talents are and they're very obvious to everyone around you too. Or you might find it difficult to believe that you have any talents at all. Maybe you've been given the message that you're stupid or useless so often that you've taken that message to heart.

Whatever we believe about how talented we are, the Bible tells us clearly that God has given each of us a special 'gift'. Paul, who wrote these words, is probably talking about God's grace and forgiveness more than anything else. But as we read on, we find that one of the effects of God's grace in our lives is that God gives each of us unique skills and talents.

So if you struggle to believe you have any kind of talent at all, take Paul's words on board. God's grace – and the talents that grace brings – is for each one of us, including you.

On the other hand, if you already know you're talented, that's great. But don't become arrogant because of that. Everyone else is talented too! Our talents shouldn't make us proud of ourselves; they should inspire us to worship the God who gave them to us and enable us to play a part in strengthening the Church (v12).

In this series of readings, we'll investigate what talent looks like and how to use our talents and make the most of them. We'll go on to think about how we can spot talents in other people and encourage them in those talents, too.

Think

What talents do you think you have? If you're not sure, ask someone who knows you well. Pray and ask God to show you more clearly what talents He has given you and how you should use them.

On purpose

READ: JEREMIAH 1:4–10

KEY VERSE V5
'Before I formed you in the womb I knew you'

There's no better feeling than doing something you really love and care about, and knowing that it's exactly what God wants you to be doing. God has created each of us differently. He made us each unique, with unique passions – and that's amazing! He's given us these passions, not only to enjoy but to glorify Him, and if we hand our passions over to Him they can reach their fullest potential.

Sometimes the way to discover our talents is to ask ourselves what motivates us; to ask what we're passionate about. That's not to say that everything we enjoy will be used by God. (A love of jelly beans is yet to be known to have brought anyone to Jesus.) But God knows us better than we know ourselves, and so we can trust Him to use what we're passionate about for His purposes.

As the key verse says, God's known us since the beginning. He knows us better than we know ourselves. God's purposes are perfect and He has made us all to do amazing but different things. If you want to discover God's purposes for you, why not start by asking what it is that gets you up in the morning?

HOT TOPIC | TALENT 1

⬆ *Pray*
Ask God to show you what your passions are, and from there to show you the talents He's given you. The answers to these questions may already be obvious!

Got skills

READ: EXODUS 31:1–11

KEY VERSE V6
'I have given ability to all the skilled workers to make everything I have commanded you'

There's something very special about a masterpiece. A truly exceptional piece of art will take your breath away when you see it. The same is true of an outstanding piece of music or a fantastically designed building. Perhaps masterpieces affect us so powerfully because God inspired the people who created these things and gave them the talents they needed to create them.

God doesn't just give us talents that we can use in church on Sunday. Yes, He does give some people gifts of teaching, evangelism and prophecy, as we saw at the weekend (Eph. 4:11), but the gifts God gives are far wider and more diverse than that. For example, in this reading from Exodus, God gives certain people skills in art, craft and metalwork. These don't sound very 'spiritual', but they were just what God wanted.

God gives us all kinds of different skills today too. Whether we're arty, sporty, academic or good at looking after other people, these talents come from Him. The challenge for us is the same as for Bezalel and Oholiab; to not be selfish with our talents but instead use them to serve God.

Think

Think about the talents God has given you. Are you using them for your own ambitions or have you devoted them to God? Commit to using those talents to serve Him. Ask for His help in doing that.

HOT TOPIC | TALENT 1

Special delivery

READ: 1 CORINTHIANS 12:1–11

KEY VERSE V1
*'Now about the gifts of the Spirit, brothers and sisters,
I do not want you to be uninformed.'*

Has someone ever given you a message from God? There
are countless testimonies of people who have had another
person, someone who had no way of knowing anything
about their situation, share something really encouraging
with them which they say came from God.

These are examples of a 'message of knowledge' (v8).
This gift and the others mentioned in 1 Corinthians 12 are
like talents, but a little different. As the name suggests,
spiritual gifts are given to us by God (v11), just like talents.
But unlike talents, we don't automatically have spiritual
gifts. While God gives everyone talents, He reserves
spiritual gifts for people who know Him and want to
follow Him. So Christians can have both! Spiritual gifts are
abilities that are only possible by the power of God, and
they're incredible. When someone uses a spiritual gift it
can be very impressive. But, just like talents, spiritual gifts
aren't for our own benefit – they're to enable us to help
other people, as verse 7 tells us.

God wants to give you spiritual gifts, and He wants to
see you use them well. Let Him fill you with the Holy Spirit
and see what happens next!

 Pray
*Ask God to fill you with the Holy Spirit. Ask Him to make you
more like Jesus and to show you what spiritual gifts He has
given you or wants to give you.*

HOT TOPIC | TALENT 1

What are you waiting for?

READ: ROMANS 12:6–8; MATTHEW 25:14–30

KEY VERSE ROMANS 12:7
'if it is serving, then serve; if it is teaching, then teach'

What's the worst present you've ever been given? Have you mastered the pretend-you-like-it face? Let's face it, there are some presents that we unwrap and decide we have no interest in, in about 2.5 seconds. We don't throw them in the bin immediately – that's too awkward and rude. We just put them at the back of a cupboard somewhere, one day to be thrown away or even re-gifted!

The gifts God gives us are much more pleasing and valuable than the presents left at the back of your cupboard. So we should make use of whatever talents we have, out of respect for other people and out of a desire to honour God.

In our second reading, Jesus tells a parable which reinforces this idea. This parable doesn't mean that if we don't use our talents, God will leave us in pain and torment forever. That's not the truth of the gospel. But the parable does tell us clearly that how we live now matters. God has blessed us in so many ways and it's our duty to use what He has given us. When we use our talents, we honour God, we help the people around us and we give them a glimpse of the God who enabled us to do what we're doing.

 Challenge
Use your talents! Think of one particular talent or skill you have (however big or small it seems) and find a way to use it regularly, so that other people can catch a glimpse of God.

HOT TOPIC | TALENT 1

Credit where credit's due

KEY VERSE V17
'Every good and perfect gift is from above, coming down from the Father'

What's the best present anyone's ever given you? How did you react to this present? Obviously it would have made you happy – maybe you were also excited to use it, and maybe you were super thankful to whoever bought it for you. But did it make you proud of yourself? Of course not. That's weird. But I bet you can think of someone who's proud of themselves because of the talents they have.

This is just as bizarre as being proud of yourself because of a present you were given or because of your height or your hair colour. We have no control over the talents we have, so being proud of our talents is ridiculous! Our talents, like every other good thing in our lives, are gifts from God. Our response to our talents should be to use them, as we've already said. But before we even do that, we should respond by acknowledging that our talents are gifts from God and by thanking Him for what He has given us.

So let's switch it up. If someone complimented our new shoes that were given to us by the person standing next to us, we'd give them the credit, so let's give God the credit when our talents get recognised.

HOT TOPIC | TALENT 1

😮 *Think*

Do you ever take your talents for granted? Do you ever fall into the trap of being proud of your talents? Decide now to be thankful to God for what He has given you.

Weekend

15/16 FEB

Glory

READ: COLOSSIANS 3:12–17

KEY VERSE V17
'And whatever you do, whether in word or deed, do it all in the name of the Lord Jesus'

If you've ever watched a football match, you'll be aware of just how out there some of the celebrations can be. For some reason, the individual who has the final say in scoring quite often takes all the recognition, running around pointing at themselves, grabbing all the glory. No matter how much the team may have done to create the opportunity for them, some scorers would rather claim all the credit for themselves.

Often, when we're good at something, it goes to our heads. We can be tempted to ignore that it was God who gave us the talent and soak up the praise ourselves. This might even be something that you don't think of as 'spiritual'. When you're complimented on something, do you give the glory to Jesus, or just enjoy the limelight? This can happen in churches as well: when someone compliments something we've done, whether playing in the band or doing a great job of welcoming people, all that glory has to be reflected back to God – the one who gave us the talent.

There are two challenges here. First, acknowledging God in all you do. This is the 'whatever you do' part of the verse (in case that didn't click). Don't pack the 'God stuff' into one corner of your life, but remember that He created all of you, and has given you talents that you can use outside the church walls. Second, we are called to acknowledge God at all times. Worship at 3am, anyone? No, this just means not using our talents for attention or an ego boost. Instead, we can use them to show how wonderful God is. All those gifts and talents come from Him, so it only seems fair to let them point back to Him! So, how could you make a start on this, this weekend?

 ## Pray

Dear God, thank You so much for the talents You've given me. Please give me opportunities to glorify Your name through these. Amen.

He's got the power

READ: 1 SAMUEL 17:32–51

KEY VERSE V45
'You come against me with sword and spear and javelin, but I come against you in the name of the LORD Almighty'

HOT TOPIC | TALENT 1

→ Perhaps the most famous story about King David is his defeat of Goliath. One swing of a slingshot and – BAM – the most fearsome foe Israel were facing was defeated. A lucky shot, a precise calculation of wind speed and trigonometry, or something bigger?

We pick up the story after David has been sent to give food to his brothers on the frontline. What's interesting about David's moment is that it comes very soon after David is anointed by Samuel (see 1 Sam. 16:1–13). There seems to be a direct relationship between God empowering someone, and that person's talents being noticed and used. And perhaps that is the point. David approached the battlefield knowing that all he had to offer came from God, knowing that from the world's perspective there was nothing particular about himself that would lead him to victory. It was just him, a stone and, most importantly, the almighty God.

In the midst of an amazing victory, David points to the one who made it happen, rather than himself. No wonder he is remembered as such a good king. It is God who gives us our talents, and when we're humble enough to acknowledge that, these talents can be used to their full potential.

 Challenge
Do you think you're humble enough with what God has given you? Try to come up with some ways to be reminded of God's greatness every day.

No comparison

READ: MATTHEW 25:14–30

KEY VERSE V21

'Well done, good and faithful servant! You have been faithful with a few things; I will put you in charge of many things.'

What are you like when given responsibilities? Do you love the feeling of being responsible for something, or do you try to avoid it at all costs?

When the master in this story returns from his journey, each servant's performance is measured in relation to what was given to him, rather than the other servants. And it's the servants who have used what he gave them that not only get a 'well done' but get even more given to them!

The challenge here is not about achieving great things, it's about using what God has given us to the full. Imagine Spider-man had spent life wishing he was Ant-man – what a waste of his gifts that would have been! If you spend your whole life ignoring the things you are brilliant at and wishing you were better in other ways, you're just wasting the talents God has given you and the life He's designed for you. God has different plans for each of us, and it's what we do with the gifts we've been given to use that matters. So stop comparing your talents to those around you. God has made you unique, with a set of talents and a plan individual to you.

HOT TOPIC | TALENT 1

Think

Do you spend too much time wishing you had other people's talents? The funny thing is there's probably someone out there who wishes they had yours! So ask yourself: am I doing enough with what God has given me?

Yoda best

READ: 1 KINGS 19:19–21

KEY VERSE V19
'Elijah went from there and found Elisha... Elijah went up to him and threw his cloak around him.'

Do you have a Yoda? Just in case you've never seen Star Wars, Yoda is a Jedi Master who helps Luke Skywalker hone his own Jedi skills. Yoda doesn't look very impressive to start with, but he turns out to be immensely wise and skilful. He helps Luke to become far stronger than he could have been on his own.

Elijah does something similar for Elisha. He notices the calling and abilities God has given Elisha, takes him under his wing, teaches him to do what he himself is doing and develops the talents God has given him. Because of this time and effort, when Elijah is finally taken into heaven, Elisha is ready to carry on Elijah's work. Elisha's experience of being mentored helps him to make the most of his God-given abilities and feel confident going forward.

It can be really helpful to have someone in your life who can be a mentor to you – someone who knows their stuff, who has similar talents to you and genuinely wants to help you grow in the skills God has given you. They can be someone who you ask your questions to, share the things you're finding difficult with, and who you know will pray for you. Who could do that for you?

Challenge
Speak to your youth leader or church leader about finding a mentor – someone with similar talents to you, who could encourage you and help you develop your skills.

HOT TOPIC | TALENT 1

Work it out

READ: PROVERBS 10:1–9

KEY VERSE V4
'Lazy hands make for poverty, but diligent hands bring wealth.'

Imagine if Jennifer Lawrence (who played Katniss Everdeen in *The Hunger Games*) had sat around at home all day, every day. Jennifer has talent, yes, but it takes hard work to put it into action. Had she not gone out and auditioned for roles, she wouldn't have the success she does now. Proverbs puts the same truth in an even punchier way: lazy people are soon poor; hard workers get rich.

Hard work might not always make us rich and successful in worldly terms, but whatever we want to achieve, hard work is vital. It's not enough just to be talented. If we want to make any kind of difference to our own situation, to the people around us or in extending God's kingdom, we must be prepared to put in the work.

So what does hard work look like? It means getting up on time. It means practising and planning. It means showing up when you've said you'll be somewhere. It means getting on with things that aren't fun but that you know will help.

Take a moment to think about your own talent. Do you invest the time, effort and energy that will allow it to flourish? To play our part in bringing God's kingdom on earth, we need to be disciplined, committed and persevering.

HOT TOPIC | TALENT 1

 Pray
Lord God, thank You for the talents You have given me. Please help me to work hard and be committed so that I can play a part in bringing Your kingdom on earth. Amen.

Who's with me?

READ: EXODUS 3:1–12

KEY VERSES VV11–12
*'But Moses said to God, "Who am I that I should go...?"
And God said, "I will be with you."'*

Moses is renowned as a great hero of the Christian and Jewish faiths. But before he did any of the great things he is known for, Moses was scared, timid and full of self-doubt. This is the Moses we meet in Exodus 3. God's response to Moses' self-doubt is fascinating. Moses asks, 'Who am I?' God replies, 'I will be with you.' God doesn't actually answer the question!

Perhaps God wanted Moses to understand that it didn't matter how important or powerful he was in his own right. God Himself would be with Moses and His power and authority would make Moses powerful and authoritative. God also deals with Moses' worries about his lack of skill as a speaker (see Exod. 4:11–12).

If we feel scared, nervous and full of self-doubt, there's encouragement for us here. None of us are anything special in ourselves, but our God is with us. He will equip us for every task He calls us to. If we feel like we can nail something without Him, we need to be careful. If Moses had tried to confront Pharaoh and lead the Israelites relying on his own abilities, he would have got into a mess. We face the same pitfall today. Whatever we do, however confident and talented we feel, let's rely on God to help us and strengthen us.

Challenge

What challenges are you facing today? Rely on God to be with you to guide you and give you wisdom and skill.

HOT TOPIC | TALENT 1

**WEEKEND
22/23 FEB**

THE TRINITY

We're all God lookalikes

READ: GENESIS 1:26–28

KEY VERSE V26
'Then God said, "Let us make mankind in our image, in our likeness"'

Welcome back to our notes on the Trinity! So far we've looked at how the Trinity shows us that God is a God of relationship. In this second section, we're going to focus on how the Trinity helps us, whether that's by revealing things to us, helping us rest or empowering us to do great things for God.

Today we start with a very important fact: God created us in His image. Genesis tells us that God created the animals, plants and trees, but He created us in His own image. Each person of God spoke to the other and decided to make human beings like themselves. So if you're wondering what God looks like – look in a mirror!

Humans are unique because we're in touch with our mind, body, emotions and spirit – and we have free choice. After a lot of exercise we are physically tired, but mentally we're really stimulated because, so scientists tell us, of all those endorphins whizzing around our bodies. However, after a long exam we can be mentally exhausted yet physically charged with the energy to run it all off. After receiving bad news, our bodies may be fine but we can feel really down emotionally. You don't see monkeys having to deal with all of this!

Our makeup reflects, in measure, the makeup of the Trinity. We were given a body to use, a brain with which to make decisions, imagine and design, and a spirit – which the Holy Trinity breathed into us with 'the breath of life' (Gen. 2:7). So whatever we lack, whatever we need, God knows because He understands us as easily as He knows Himself! Wow!

Pray

Lord, thank You that You have created me in Your image. Thank You for all You've given me to serve You with – my mind, body, emotions and spirit. And thank You for knowing and understanding me completely. Amen.

Like father, like son

READ: COLOSSIANS 1:15–23

KEY VERSE V15
'The Son is the image of the invisible God, the firstborn over all creation.'

Not everyone takes after their parents. You might meet some really rude and unpleasant people who have really kind, hard-working and loving parents. Maybe one of your best friends is great fun to be around, generous and patient – but had a really difficult upbringing and parents who were perhaps uncaring or largely absent.

Paul tells the church in Colosse that Jesus is just like His Dad. If they want to know what God is like, they only need to look at Jesus. Jesus is more than a good man, a healer, a storyteller, a wise man, a prophet, a freedom fighter or a politician. Paul tells us that Jesus is the image of the invisible God.

It is important for us to understand that Jesus isn't similar to or just a bit like God. He is the exact image of God. He reflects God. Jesus is God, God is Jesus. So we can know and understand God better through reading accounts of Jesus in the Bible. And as we read yesterday, we are also made in the image of God, so we can understand ourselves better too! Jesus knows our human temptations and struggles first-hand. And because He is God, He knows the best way to help us through anything.

CORE THEME | THE TRINITY 2

66 *Share*

'One thing I know about God is that He's perfect. One thing I know about Jesus is that He's selfless. One thing I know about the Holy Spirit is that He's everywhere.' (Jacob, 16)

It's a fact

READ: JOHN 10:22–36

KEY VERSE V29
'My Father... has given them to me... no one can snatch them out of my Father's hand.'

Blasphemy is not showing proper reverence to God. In biblical times, the punishment for blasphemy was death by stoning (Lev. 24:13–16). Jesus knew these laws but He also knew that people needed to hear the truth about who He was and is.

Jesus couldn't have been more clear and upfront with the crowd if He'd tried. 'I and the Father are one' (v30), He told an angry mob, who then picked up stones to kill Him. This statement would have so angered the crowd – they would have heard it as blatant blasphemy. But Jesus was stating a fact: He is a member of the Trinity. The crowd could choose to believe that fact or not!

Jesus and the Father are one. Nothing that Jesus does is without the Father's say-so and the Spirit's guidance and direction. They work in perfect harmony together.

We also read today about 'sheep'. The sheep are Jesus' followers – you and me! Jesus says we can know His voice and be directed by Him, but more, He says that no one can take us away from God. Isn't this an amazing and comforting word for today? Whenever we feel weak, anxious or confused, we can rest and feel secure in this promise.

CORE THEME | THE TRINITY 2

❝ *Share*

'One thing I know about God is that He's God. One thing I know about Jesus is that He's real. One thing I know about the Holy Spirit is that He's with me.' (Daniel, 15)

Random acts of kindness

READ: TITUS 3:4–8

KEY VERSES VV4–5
'when the kindness and love of God our Saviour appeared, he saved us'

Who is the kindest person you know? One of your teachers or leaders at church? Or maybe it's one of your friends, parents or grandparents, or even a well-known celebrity? In what ways are they kind to you or other people? The people of New Zealand have a reputation for being the kindest people on Earth. They are known to be welcoming and always ready to help – what a reputation to have!

When Paul writes to Titus, he describes God as a kind God. Kindness is described in the dictionary as a friendly, generous, helpful, considerate and loving quality, act or behaviour. This definition can really help us to understand the different aspects of the Trinity.

The quality of kindness can be linked to the Father who, even from before the foundation of the world, had prepared a rescue plan to save humankind from sin. This act of kindness saw the God of the universe shrink down by the Spirit's power into a tiny embryo, being born as a helpless human baby into very humble circumstances.

We can have the same behaviour as Jesus through the Holy Spirit living in us, giving us the power to live as He lived, to be kind as He was kind.

➕ *Challenge*
Jesus is the perfect example of the kindness of God. Here's our challenge for today: how can you show a random act of kindness to someone? (Could you try to show it without them knowing it was you?)

CORE THEME | THE TRINITY 2

Emotional rollercoaster

READ: ACTS 2:1–12

KEY VERSE V4
'All of them were filled with the Holy Spirit and began to speak in other tongues'

It had been an emotional few weeks for Jesus' closest friends. They had been crushed when their Lord had been crucified; overjoyed when they saw that He was alive again; and then saddened when they saw Him leave and ascend to heaven. Now, they were hiding away from the world, waiting on God for whatever would happen next, not knowing quite what to expect. They were probably feeling a little abandoned, confused and sorry for themselves. They hadn't understood that Jesus had to return to the Father in order to send the Spirit. These faithful, tired and emotionally drained friends were about to experience a major spiritual boost!

Today's reading is about the very first outpouring of the Holy Spirit after Jesus returned to heaven. It was also the first and probably greatest evangelistic event ever seen! Suddenly, God gives them all His Holy Spirit, enabling a rough bunch of Galilean men, including fishermen and a tax collector, to speak in 15 different languages or more. There's no mention of fear at this point. The scene drew an enormous crowd, including Parthians, Medes, Elamites, Egyptians, Romans, Cretans and Arabs, who marvelled at what was going on.

66 Share

'One thing I know about God is that He created all things. One thing I know about Jesus is that He died on the cross. One thing I know about the Holy Spirit is that He uses people to do things.' (Cam, 15)

CORE THEME | THE TRINITY 2

We can't but He can

READ: GENESIS 41:38–40

KEY VERSE V38
'Can we find anyone like this man, one in whom is the spirit of God?'

Captain America, the *Marvel* superhero, wasn't always strong and powerful. Before he took an experimental serum, he was just plain Steve Rogers – a small and frail-looking young man. The Holy Spirit is not a serum but He does help us to do things that we couldn't do on our own.

Joseph had experienced a tough few years. He had been sold to traders by his jealous brothers, endured years of slavery, was wrongly accused by his master's wife and then left to rot in prison. He had no status, family, freedom or power of any sort. But then one day, Joseph was summoned into the Pharaoh's presence and asked to interpret a dream that had confused all the wise men of Egypt. Amazingly, Joseph responds: 'I cannot do it... but God will give Pharaoh the answer he desires' (Gen. 41:16). The Spirit enabled Joseph to interpret the dream.

Before Pentecost (which we read about yesterday), the Spirit of God was only given to individuals at key times: David to write songs, Elijah to perform miracles, Samson to judge Israel and a shy, feeble Gideon to defeat the Midianites! During these times, He always brought glory and honour to His name.

💬 *Share*

'One thing I know about God is that He's all powerful. One thing I know about Jesus is that He's the Son of God. One thing I know about the Holy Spirit is that He gives us gifts.'
(Josh, 16)

CORE THEME | THE TRINITY 2

Weekend

29 FEB/1 MAR

The penny drops

READ: 1 CORINTHIANS 2:1–16

KEY VERSE V10
'these are the things God has revealed to us by his Spirit.'

Have you ever been told by a friend, 'You must see this film' or 'You must get this album'?

A lot of socialising is about sharing the latest gadgets, music, games and fashion. Your friends reveal their lives to you – the things they enjoy – and, in turn, you do the same. A whole new world of a certain genre of fiction, type of music or sport has opened up to you. Sharing our interests deepens our relationships and connects us with each other – and we were created for relationship.

In today's passage, we see that the Holy Spirit also reveals things to us. Some of the wisest, cleverest people in the world cannot understand the wisdom of God or the nature of our free salvation in Jesus. Yet a five-year-old can completely understand that Jesus loves them and has died for them. It is not a matter of intelligence, but rather a matter of the Spirit revealing this truth to us. We didn't work it out for ourselves, instead the Spirit opens our eyes and hearts. The penny drops and everything starts to make sense.

God speaks through His Spirit into the lives of humankind. He reveals the truth about Jesus' death for our sins, His resurrection and His ascension. He softens the hardest hearts and opens the blindest eyes, all because He loves each one of us more than we could ever imagine. He reveals things to us for the same reason we share things with each other – He wants to be closer to us, and He wants us to feel closer to Him.

Challenge

Have you been trying hard to convince your friends about the truth of Christianity, but without success? Ask the Holy Spirit to reveal the love of God to your friends through your everyday conversations.

No sacrifice required

≡ **READ: 1 CORINTHIANS 12:1–11**

KEY VERSE V4
'There are different kinds of gifts, but the same Spirit distributes them.'

How well do you know Roman mythology? The Romans had a lot of gods and goddesses, each responsible for different areas or things. For example, Venus is the goddess of love and beauty; Mars is the god of war; Pluto is the god of the underworld, and Minerva is the goddess of wisdom. During the time that Paul was writing, Jews were familiar with the Romans asking different gods for different things. Roman worshippers would give sacrifices in the hope that the god would favour them in return.

Paul is careful to point out to the Corinthians that there is only one Holy Spirit – not many spirits of God. There is only one Spirit who gives to people all the gifts at His discretion. Paul refers to the Spirit as He, not because the Spirit looks or feels like a He, but because the Spirit of God is an entity; another equal member of the Trinity. Paul also tells us that the Spirit has intelligence, with a mind and will, and that He gives gifts to whomever He chooses. We don't need to offer sacrifices or perform some ritual, we can just pray to Him and He will generously bless us with what we need. Why not try praying to the Holy Spirit? He is ready and waiting to hear from you right now.

CORE THEME | THE TRINITY 2

Think
When you pray to God, do you often speak to the Holy Spirit? If not, try to get to know Him better through talking to Him and reading about Him.

Different but united

READ: 1 CORINTHIANS 12:7–27

KEY VERSE V7
'Now to each one the manifestation of the Spirit is given for the common good.'

In the UK, we are fortunate to have access to the NHS for any medical needs. According to gov.uk, there are 1.2 million staff employed by the NHS, working in different departments and at all sorts of levels. A fifth of the staff are from Asian, Black, Chinese, and other ethnic groups – lots of different people who work for one organisation so that our bodies can get the care they need.

In explaining the gifts of the Spirit, Paul uses the analogy of a body. Each part has equal importance, even though they are very different and operate in a unique way. The eye, foot and head are obviously all very different, but so vital if the body is to function properly.

The Holy Spirit gives gifts as He sees necessary: the gift of being wise, the gift of strong faith and, to some, the gift of healing others. The reason for the gifts is not just to encourage and help the individual receiver to grow in Christ; the gifts of the Holy Spirit are given to the body of Christ (that is, the Church) for its encouragement and growth.

Let's ask the Holy Spirit to give us gifts that we can use to build up the worldwide Church – and be Jesus' hands and feet on the earth.

CORE THEME | THE TRINITY 2

 Pray

Dear Holy Spirit, thank You that You know me so well. I pray that You will give me gifts that suit my personality and that I can use to draw others to know Your amazing love. Amen.

67

Fruit salad

READ: GALATIANS 5:13–25

KEY VERSES VV22–23
'But the fruit of the Spirit is love, joy, peace, forbearance, kindness, goodness, faithfulness, gentleness and self-control.'

A fruit is the sweet or fleshy part of a tree or plant that contains seed and can be eaten as food. We all know that apples, satsumas, peaches and strawberries are fruits. But did you know that so are tomatoes, cucumbers and peppers? Imagine having tomatoes and peppers in your fruit salad!

Yesterday we looked at the gifts of the Spirit given to different people to build up the Church – the body of Christ. The fruit of the Spirit is a little different to His gifts. It is seen in our character rather than in what we do for others. Like a tiny apple tree that produces full-sized apples, we produce fruit if we put our roots into God and His Word.

In turn, our fruit gives glory back to the Father through the work of the Son, because people begin to make the connection between the way we live our lives and who we believe in (Jesus). Hopefully, people will then want to learn about God and why He sent Jesus to die for us.

As the Spirit lives in us, He encourages us to give up our old lives and live a new, fruitful life of love, joy, peace, patience, kindness, goodness, faithfulness, gentleness and self-control.

Challenge

Which fruit of the Spirit do you need more of in your life at the moment? Ask the Holy Spirit to fill you and help you, and see how you get on over the next few days!

CORE THEME | THE TRINITY 2

No water. No life.

READ: JOHN 7:30–39

KEY VERSE V37
'Let anyone who is thirsty come to me and drink.'

Have you ever been more than just merely thirsty – absolutely parched? There's nothing that can beat it when you eventually get that drink – especially if it's ice-cold, fresh water.

As He stands before the Pharisees, Jesus offers a drink to anyone who is thirsty – not physically but spiritually thirsty. Jesus says to the crowd that He is the source of this spiritual drink which anyone can receive.

The only way for someone to receive this spiritual drink (which is the Holy Spirit) is by believing in the Son. The Father will then give the believer the Spirit through the Son, Jesus – an example of the Trinity at work in our Christian life. In today's reading, Jesus is offering the Holy Spirit to anyone (not just to prophets, kings and holy people) who will simply ask Him and believe in Him.

We can become thirsty as Christians if we let our relationship with God dry up. We can feel parched, uninspired, unmotivated and unmoved. When we find ourselves feeling this way, let's go to the source who can fill us afresh today with 'rivers of living water'!

66 *Share*

'One thing I know about God is that He loves me no matter what. One thing I know about Jesus is that He died to forgive my sins. One thing I know about the Holy Spirit is that He's always with me.' (Grace, 14)

CORE THEME | THE TRINITY 2

69

Have a sit down and a cup of tea

READ: HEBREWS 10:1–18

KEY VERSE V12
'when [Jesus] had offered for all time one sacrifice for sins, he sat down at the right hand of God'

OK, so you might not be in full-time employment just yet, but have you ever worked really hard on a temporary job, or on homework or revision? After a day of hard grafting, it feels good to sit down and relax – it's satisfying, isn't it?

Well, this is the sort of feeling behind the Old Testament imagery used in today's reading. After His once and for all sacrifice, Jesus sits down at the right hand of the Father because, as He said on the cross, 'It is finished' (John 19:30). The Trinity had achieved the master plan of saving the human race from the power of sin. So Jesus returned to His rightful place with the Father in heaven, and the Spirit testifies to this truth by revealing it to all humankind through the inspired words of the Bible. Here again we see the Father, Jesus and Spirit working and resting in perfect harmony.

Every member of the Trinity is needed to ensure our salvation, redemption and invitation to follow God. We need belief in the Son's mission, belief in the Father who sent His only Son, and belief in the Spirit's words revealed through the gospel message.

Think

God knows the importance of rest – and of resting in the company of others. Think about this coming weekend and how you'll have time to rest and recharge for the next week. Could you set aside some time to spend resting with God?

**WEEKEND
7/8 MAR**

FRIENDSHIP

I'm on your team!
READ: PROVERBS 12:25–26

KEY VERSE V25
'Anxiety weighs down the heart,
but a kind word cheers it up.'

Social media has its pros and cons. It can be great for sharing what's going on in our lives with our friends, but it can also turn into a huge burden. How many 'likes' we get on a post can be a complete mood-changer. Seeing the seemingly perfect (and heavily filtered) lives of others can leave us feeling like we're lacking. We often feel we need to keep people's opinions of us high, worrying about what they'll think of us.

Within our friendships, it's really important that we are sources of encouragement. Everyone needs it. We might be aware of particular friends who are going through difficulties and could really use our kind words and support. Then there are other friends who still need this, but perhaps don't show it in ways that we immediately recognise. And there's no doubt that we ourselves love to receive encouragement, and thrive off it. This kind of encouragement isn't just a quick 'like' or a carefully selected emoji; it's thoughtful, consistent, 'I'm on your team' type stuff.

Being a young person is tough, but as friends we are called to encourage each other – which can make a huge difference. However, as we're only human ourselves, we also need people who can encourage us when we are hurting. This way everyone is supported and encouraged, and no one in our circle of friends feels alone. Let's also not forget the words Jesus said in Matthew 11: 28: 'Come to me, all you who are weary and burdened, and I will give you rest.'

Pray

Father God, please help me to be the kind of friend that You want me to be. Help me to be an encourager to my friends and family even when times are tough, and even when I am low. I know You won't give me more than I can bear. Amen.

Influencers

READ: 2 TIMOTHY 3:1–17

KEY VERSES VV2,4
'People will be lovers of themselves... rather than lovers of God'

How many friends or followers do you have on your social media accounts? Do you actually know all these people? Is it possible that you're being influenced by the sort of posts they put out? Well, the answer is 'yes' – in fact, some social media sensations would even use 'influencer' as their job title! Why? Because the more time we spend around people, online or offline, the more we become like them.

The danger here is that if we choose to associate with someone without really knowing what kind of person they are, we can find that they influence us very negatively. Often, we don't even realise it until much later when we've taken on certain traits that we wish we hadn't.

Today's reading shows what Paul wrote to Timothy about this issue. Paul knew that a lot of the people around Timothy would influence him and his church very badly, so he warned Timothy to stay away from them. As Paul says in another of his letters, 'Bad company corrupts good character' (1 Cor. 15:33).

We could learn from this advice in today's reading. Let's be cautious about who we allow to influence us. Not being unkind or rude, but just choosing to go a different way.

HOT TOPIC | FRIENDSHIP 2

Challenge

Look at the people you're friends with at the moment. Do you consider yourself to be similar to them in many ways? Are your friends influencing you positively or negatively?

Break the circle

READ: 1 THESSALONIANS 5:12–22

KEY VERSE V15
'Make sure that nobody pays back wrong for wrong, but always strive to do what is good for each other'

Have you ever heard the term 'a vicious circle'? It can be so frustrating when we see things happening like this: like a merry-go-round that just will not stop! For example, you have a disagreement with a friend and it turns into a serious argument. The argument causes a rift between the two of you and makes it even less likely that one of you will back down. Then you disagree about whose fault it all was and what you both should do about it, and the vicious circle continues. The argument just goes around and around with no sign of being resolved.

When we have disagreements with our friends, we can choose to break the vicious circle. We can be the solution to the problem! In today's reading, Paul gives us some valuable advice for healthy friendships and healthy churches. In particular, it's important to offer love and compassion, not to pay back wrong for wrong, even when we feel a friend has really wronged us, and to always seek to live in peace. The Bible tells us that 'Blessed are the peacemakers, for they will be called children of God' (Matt. 5:9). Go be a peacemaker and change the world.

Think

Just imagine what could happen if you were to back down from an argument. It's not always important to be right all the time. Backing down does not make you wrong but does create peace. Next time, try it!

HOT TOPIC | FRIENDSHIP 2

Rise above it

READ: JOB 19:13–19

KEY VERSE V19

'All my intimate friends detest me; those I love have turned against me.'

Has a friend ever turned their back on you? One day they were your friend and then the next they seemed to have turned against you. You might never understand why this happened. Was it something I said? Was it something I did or didn't do? How can I make it better? Job asks some of these questions of his friends. When everything around him is falling apart he hopes his friends will support him, but they don't.

When this happens, it's very hard to keep things in perspective. When a friend hurts us, we may want to hurt them back. When they spread rumours, we may want to retaliate. These things might seem appealing at the time, but they're not the best way to respond. In today's reading, Job calls out to God and tells Him all his worries. He complains to God and grieves over his situation. God can take all our emotions on the chin and still love us. Our God is big enough to know what are valid points and what is just moaning.

God offers us a relationship in which we can be honest about everything and still be able to call Him our friend. If we're feeling hurt and abandoned, we can go to Him. He'll never turn His back on us.

HOT TOPIC | FRIENDSHIP 2

➕ *Challenge*

When friends turn their back on you, don't lash out. Instead, take the problem to God and choose not to retaliate. It might be difficult to choose to do things this way, but it will be so worth it.

Calling...

READ: PSALM 55:1–23

KEY VERSES VV12–13
'If an enemy were insulting me, I could endure it... But it is you, a man like myself'

It's not easy handling our emotions when friends turn on us. It can be hard to keep our words reasonable and our thoughts pure. After all, we are only human and when humans get hurt, they tend to try to protect themselves. Unfortunately, this can land us in hot water! Our human nature sometimes makes us want to hurt people back, to make them suffer, to spread rumours about them or to share their secrets with others. When we are hurt, we can think that hurting the person responsible will make us feel better.

But this is not the way that God wants us to live. Yes, people will hurt us at many points in our lives. Yes, even friends may turn on us and that can be very painful. But God never lets us down and never lets us go. When we hurt, God hurts with us.

David was hurting. His closest friend was now the one who taunted him. His world was turning upside down. So, what did he do? In the middle of his pain, he turned to God and trusted in Him: 'As for me, I call to God, and the Lᴏʀᴅ saves me' (v16). No matter what happens in our friendships, God is with us and is waiting for us to call on Him. You wouldn't be the first person He's listened to talking about their friendship problems.

HOT TOPIC | FRIENDSHIP 2

Think
How do you handle being hurt or betrayed by people who were once your friends? Do you react in a negative way or do you take it to God?

True or false?

READ: PROVERBS 26:17–28

KEY VERSE V28

'A lying tongue hates those it hurts, and a flattering mouth works ruin.'

It's the worst feeling, hearing that one of your friends has stabbed you in the back, isn't it? At times, we may discover that people who called themselves our friends turn out to be false friends. When this happens, the pain can be very deep. We may have trusted them greatly, told them things we haven't told others and been generous with our money, our time and our possessions. There is no easy fix when someone turns out to be a false friend. Usually only time and God's comfort heal the wounds. But, unfortunately, false friends do exist. So, how can you spot them?

When someone's actions don't add up to what they say – when they flatter you, compliment you and then do something that hurts you – beware. No amount of flowery words can cover up constant bad behaviour towards you. A two-faced friend isn't really a friend at all, and if this keeps happening then it might be time to walk away.

It can be difficult to walk away from someone who you thought was your friend, especially if you see your friendship with them as a big part of your life. Times like these remind us to depend on God – the one who comforts us in our pain and is as real as it gets.

HOT TOPIC | FRIENDSHIP 2

Pray

Lord God, give me wisdom to tell good friends from false friends. Help me to support and encourage the friends that I have; to really value them and not hurt them. Amen.

Weekend

14/15 MAR

Watch your mouth!

READ: COLOSSIANS 4:2–6

KEY VERSE V6
'Let your conversation be always full of grace, seasoned with salt, so that you may know how to answer everyone.'

Do you ever talk with your group of friends and get so carried away with the conversation that you end up saying something you know you shouldn't have? It might have been that you betrayed a secret or said something really mean about someone. You know it's not right, but it felt so easy at the time and made you feel a little bit more on their level.

In 2 Corinthians 5:20, Paul also says, 'We are therefore Christ's ambassadors'. In politics, ambassadors are people who represent their own country in another country. They work to resolve issues and speak on behalf of their home nation. So being Jesus' ambassadors means that it's really important for us to remember that we represent Him in our conversations with our friends. The words we use can be very powerful, and whether we're aware of it or not, our friends do take notice of what comes out of our mouths as Christians.

Often we think that we have to make Christianity cool, and so say something we know we shouldn't. We think it might make us, or even God, more relatable. In our reading today, Paul tells us that it's doing exactly the opposite that is most effective. We're told to watch what we say and make sure it is always wise and full of grace, so that no one can say, 'You're a Christian. You shouldn't talk like that!' It's as people see that we're different to them that they will be interested in our faith. Being different intrigues people, and being full of grace and kindness attracts people – and this is when great conversations about Jesus could come up.

➕ Challenge

Over the next few days, each time you're about to see your friends, ask for God to help you speak in a way that is full of grace and reflects Him more. See what happens as you head into conversations this way.

Can I be honest with you?

READ: PROVERBS 27:10–17

KEY VERSE V17
'As iron sharpens iron, so one person sharpens another.'

Who would you say is your closest friend? It's great to have someone to talk to and have fun with. Someone who you have in-jokes with that nobody else stands a chance of understanding. Someone who finishes off your sentences. Someone who has your back and who you know will be there for you. But does that mean they have to agree with everything you do? No way!

A good friend is not someone who necessarily thinks that whatever we do and say is OK; it's somebody who lovingly challenges us to be a better person. They will genuinely want the best for us and will be prepared to help us with that. Just as we can be influenced negatively by friends, we can influence and be influenced in incredible ways that help to make others and ourselves more like Jesus, and this is part of God's plan for friendship.

Having friends that we can have healthy and loving disagreements with is so valuable and worth investing our time and efforts in. We grow in maturity when we can test our thoughts and ideas against another person, and when we're open to correction when we're wrong.

Think

Are you and your friends able to lovingly challenge one another to be better people? Are there people who could be friends like this to you? Look out for people like this and be willing to be this kind of friend yourself.

HOT TOPIC | FRIENDSHIP 2

Tough love

READ: PROVERBS 27:1–6

KEY VERSE V6
'Wounds from a friend can be trusted'

Sometimes it's the things our real, true friends pull us up on that hurt the most. When we trust someone and they challenge us in an area, we know it's not malicious but because they actually think it could be becoming an issue for us – and that isn't easy to hear. It can be tempting to get annoyed at them, relay a list of criticisms about them, or just ignore them altogether.

However, as we discovered yesterday, part of being in a good friendship is being able to challenge one another in loving ways that help build us up. And that's not always done with ease. It takes a lot of courage to call out a friend on something they're doing. It would be a whole lot easier for the person to just keep their mouth zipped and not bother at all. But because they really want you to be the best you can be, they do it. Isn't that great?

Once our attention has been drawn to something, we then have the opportunity to put it right – something we may not have even considered before. So let's be thankful for these challenges from friends. They may hurt at the time and make us uncomfortable, but we'll be much better off because of them.

Challenge

Perhaps your friends have been exactly what they were supposed to be: honest! Challenge yourself to be more honest with your friends this week, giving them opportunities to do the same for you.

HOT TOPIC | FRIENDSHIP 2

Let it go

READ: PROVERBS 17:1–10

KEY VERSE V9
'Love prospers when a fault is forgiven, but dwelling on it separates close friends.' (NLT)

HOT TOPIC | FRIENDSHIP 2

⟶ There's something really important that needs to be mentioned: forgiveness. Even our good friends will mess up. We will mess up. The question is, how do we move forward once this has happened?

The world around us very rarely shows forgiveness. We see people and countries at war, politicians pulling each other down and websites taking any opportunity to destroy a celebrity's reputation. It's rare to see a glimpse of forgiveness when the finger is constantly being pointed at someone. However, forgiveness is right at the centre of Christianity, of what Jesus did for us, and that makes it important.

Forgiveness is often difficult. Some people will simply say that we need to make up with the person who hurt us. It's not always that easy. Forgiveness is not just a handshake and a 'Let's forget it'. It doesn't mean that what the person did is OK. Forgiveness is about acknowledging a fault but deliberately letting it go, rather than holding a grudge.

Dwelling on things destroys, letting go restores. People have faults – lots of them. But when we choose not to hold someone's faults against them, love prospers.

Pray
Lord God, at times I get it wrong. I let You and my friends down. Help me to deal with any problems with my friends. Please forgive me and show me what it is to truly forgive others. Amen.

Double standards

READ: MATTHEW 18:21–35

KEY VERSE V33
'Shouldn't you have had mercy on your fellow servant just as I had on you?'

This story Jesus tells shows a man who had different standards for different situations. In one situation he was the person who needed to be treated with generosity and so hoped to be treated with kindness. In the next situation he was asked to be the one to show kindness and generosity, but he didn't act in this way. Instead of showing the kindness he'd been shown, he chose to treat his debtor harshly. So Jesus' challenge to us is clear: do we always treat others as we would hope to be treated?

Sometimes we can treat those closest to us the harshest! As we are familiar with them, we can fall into the trap of thinking that it's OK to be hard on them, because they will forgive us. God teaches us that acting this way will only backfire on us. We're reminded that He has forgiven us a great deal, so we must be willing to show forgiveness to others, including our friends. If we need kindness from God, we should show the same kindness to other people. On top of all that, if we want good friends we need to be a good friend, acting in ways that we hope they will act towards us, not expecting more from them than we are willing to give.

Pray
Lord God, help me to get things right with my friends. Help me to offer kindness and forgiveness to all of them, just as You have shown kindness and forgiveness to me. Amen.

HOT TOPIC | FRIENDSHIP 2

Unlikely friends

READ: MATTHEW 5:43–48

KEY VERSE V47
'And if you greet only your own people, what are you doing more than others?'

Have you ever written someone off just because of the way they looked or acted? Are there some people that you refuse to hang around with just because they're not part of your group and are a bit different?

We often pass up opportunities to connect with people because we assume that they're too different from us. But if we behave like this how are we different from people who don't know Jesus? Jesus welcomed and accepted everyone; including those other people didn't want to know. Following Jesus means doing what He did and choosing to show friendship – even to people who don't 'fit in'. Sometimes these can make for the most meaningful friendships, because they're not superficial in any way.

If we only hang around with people who look like us, act like us and talk like us, not only are we missing out on an opportunity to be like Jesus, we're missing out on an opportunity to explore more of life and the wonderful, different people that God has created.

As we finish this series, remember that making friends doesn't mean forming a clique. It means showing Jesus' love and acceptance to people very different from ourselves.

Think

How ready are you to show friendship to people who are different from you? Who might Jesus want you to befriend? Pray about this and ask Jesus to help you accept everyone, just as He does.

**WEEKEND
21/22 MAR**

DISCIPLINE

You're grounded!

READ: PROVERBS 19:16–21

KEY VERSE V18
'Discipline your children, for in that there is hope'

Think of a small child being taught to cross the road safely by an adult. No doubt we all had this kind of instruction when we were younger. But why? What is the purpose of teaching a child to cross the road with care? Surely it is to ensure that they stay safe and that, in time, they will be able to cross the road independently without fear of getting hurt.

Discipline is about being taught to be wiser and more responsible. Most people, when they discipline us, do it for our own good (or at least that is their hope). They do it because they care about us and want the best for us. That doesn't stop us,

however, from sometimes finding discipline hard to take. We like to think that we are pretty intelligent people who can do a good job of looking out for ourselves. But those who love and care for us have a duty to look out for us, and to discipline us where necessary.

A blunt pencil is made sharper and regains its usefulness only by having bits shaved off. A rose bush can only continue to grow healthily and more beautifully when it is pruned. Sometimes, the process of being disciplined can be really tough – no one actually *wants* to be grounded or have no allowance. But it helps if we view this discipline differently: someone who cares about us is helping us to become the person we ultimately should be, knowing that they're probably going to have to bear the brunt of our annoyance. They're making a choice to help us know the right way to go about life.

Pray

Father God, please help me to respond positively to discipline and to see it as a way of growing. Help me to accept discipline graciously and willingly from those who love and care for me. Amen.

We're breaking free

READ: JOHN 8:21–32

KEY VERSE V31
'Jesus said, "If you hold to my teaching, you are really my disciples."'

Have you noticed that the word 'discipline' is very similar to the word 'disciple'? Apparently, our word 'disciple' comes from the Latin for 'learner' and the word 'discipline' means 'instruction' or 'teaching'. To be a follower of Jesus is to follow and learn from His teachings. Or, to put it another way, to be a disciple of Jesus is to be subject to His discipline.

When we think of it in this way, discipline isn't such a negative concept. Rather, it is something we should strive for. If we want to be genuine followers of Jesus, then we need to follow His teachings and instructions. In other words, we need to experience His discipline.

Today's Bible reading highlights that by being His disciples we can enjoy freedom as a result of knowing the truth (v32). We often think of discipline as something that limits us, stopping us from doing the things we would like to do. Over the next couple of weeks, we'll explore the idea that discipline actually helps us to be free so that we can enjoy life more. Jesus said that he wants to give us 'life... to the full' (John 10:10). Following His way of doing things, His discipline, is our way to getting our hands on that.

HOT TOPIC | DISCIPLINE 2

Think

Do you think of discipline as being negative? In what ways do you think discipline might enable us to be freer? How might God discipline us?

Delightful discipline?

 READ: PROVERBS 3:11–20

KEY VERSE V12
'the Lᴏʀᴅ disciplines those he loves, as a father the son he delights in.'

A couple of days ago we mentioned that parents usually discipline their children because they love them and want the best for them. We often talk of God as being our Father and, therefore, it's inevitable that He should have a role in disciplining us. Yet, for many of us, if we stop and think of God disciplining us, it can be hard to pinpoint what that actually involves. Does God punish us by striking us down with a dreadful illness or making it rain all day when we want it to be sunny? In reality, this is not usually the case. However, the Bible often assures us that God does indeed discipline us. But today's reading points out that we shouldn't be unhappy about receiving the discipline that God gives out. Instead, we should see it as a big reminder of how much He loves us and even 'delights' in us, so much that He wants us to gain wisdom so that we can live our best lives.

Over the next few days we'll be digging into some key Bible passages that look at this, and thinking a bit more about what it means to be disciplined by God, what that looks like, and how we can respond.

 Pray

Thank You, Father, that You love us as Your children and want the best for us. Help us to accept Your discipline and be reminded that it is so that we can become better followers of You. Amen.

HOT TOPIC | DISCIPLINE 2

Facing the music

READ: 2 SAMUEL 12:1–12

KEY VERSE V11
'Out of your own household I am going to bring calamity on you.'

Let's have a bit of background, in case you're not familiar with the story. King David had fallen for a woman who was already married. David slept with her, despite being well aware that this was wrong, and she became pregnant. In the end, David resorted to having her husband murdered so that he could marry the woman and avoid a scandal.

In Nathan's story, which we read today, David is confronted with what he did. When we know we've done wrong, the very best thing we can do is face up to it, acknowledge what we've done and learn from it.

Although we can be forgiven by God when we sin, as Nathan later tells David he has been once David acknowledged his sin, this does not free us from the negative consequences of what we've done. This is why learning to obey God and choosing well is so important.

How many times have you prayed something like this: 'God, I'm sorry. Please let everything go back to normal'? If God answered this prayer in the way we would like every time we prayed it, we probably wouldn't ever learn from our mistakes. It is only by facing up to the consequences, knowing that God loves and forgives us, that we are able to move on.

HOT TOPIC | DISCIPLINE 2

Pray
Thank You, Father God, that You forgive us when we come to You in repentance. Help us to learn from the consequences of our mistakes so that we choose differently in future. Amen.

It pays off

≡ **READ: ROMANS 6:12–23**

KEY VERSE V22
'But now that you have been set free from sin and have become slaves of God'

HOT TOPIC | DISCIPLINE 2

If someone is in authority over you, does it mean that you have to do everything they tell you to do? In most circumstances, probably not. We have free will and, because of that, can decide whether or not to do what a parent, carer, teacher or other person in authority asks us to do. However, we will face the consequences of any decision we take, so what might they be?

Sometimes, when we are too stubborn to do what someone who loves us asks us to do, we miss out on a possible good consequence. Can you think of a time when this could have happened to you? Maybe there's been a time when someone has surprised you with something, but in order for the surprise to not get ruined, you had to follow what that person said – and you're glad you did.

Today's Bible reading makes no secret or surprise out of the reward for trusting in Jesus and obeying God – it puts it plainly: the reward is eternal life. This is in contrast to the pain that results from being a slave to sin, constantly caught up in it. When we see our two options, there's no competition really! It's pays off to listen to what God has to say.

Challenge

Is God calling you to do something in particular, or to give something up? Are you resisting Him in this? Take a brave step today and decide to obey Him. It might be scary, but it'll definitely be worth it.

Through the fire

READ: 1 PETER 1:3–9

KEY VERSE V7
'These have come so that the proven genuineness of your faith... may result in praise, glory and honour'

One way in which we can receive discipline and be made more into the people God wants us to be is by being allowed to go through difficult times. You may remember that last weekend we talked about the need for pencils to be sharpened and rose bushes to be pruned. If you were trying to purify a metal, such as gold, you would subject it to high temperatures. This would help you to refine it and to separate the impurities from the molten gold.

Today's verses tell us that our faith can be refined by going through trials. When we face difficulties, we rely more on God and we think really seriously about our priorities. But we're not alone as we face trials. Our Lord Jesus faced the ultimate trial when He went to the cross to die for us. How horrible that must have been – to suffer so much when He did not deserve to. But what an amazing outcome it had. Jesus defeated death and restored humankind's relationship with God! So as you face trials in your life, remember this: Jesus understands and you will come out of the refining fire stronger and more mature than you were before. Cling on to that.

Think

How do you feel when you are going through a difficult time? Can you look back at times in your life that have been hard and see how God has strengthened you and brought you closer to Him through them?

Weekend

28/29 MAR

No guidance

READ: PROVERBS 5:1–14

KEY VERSE V12
'You will say, "How I hated discipline! How my heart spurned correction!"'

How do you feel if you are told off? Some people are quick to apologise, some laugh, some get angry and shout back, and some even run away.

Not many of us like being disciplined, and we may be tempted to ignore those who try to set us straight. But just take a minute to imagine what might happen if we didn't have our mistakes pointed out and made clear to us. Watching someone make bad decisions can be like watching a horrific crash in slow motion.

Today's reading highlights that those people who choose to ignore wise instruction usually live to regret it. Let's think about drugs, for example. Parents, teachers and youth workers tell us not to do them – but for some, that's not enough to swerve the temptation. However, fast forward ten years to someone who's addicted to drugs and has seen the devastating effects of this on their life, and they would probably wish they'd listened to the instructions they were given.

That's an extreme example but the point is that discipline and instruction are given to us for a reason. At the time, we might think the only use they have is killing our fun, but if we ignore them we can end up in sticky situations, really regretting it.

 ## Challenge

How do you respond to discipline? What might be the consequences if you choose to ignore those who try to help you by disciplining you?

Don't ditch the rules

 READ: PROVERBS 5:21–23

KEY VERSE V22
'The evil deeds of the wicked ensnare them; the cords of their sins hold them fast.'

There are times when we might quite like the idea of life without the restrictions that rules bring. Many people like to tell us that rules are there to be broken. But can you imagine a school without rules or a society with no laws?

Imagine that you and a group of your friends sailed off to a desert island and established a new community. Very quickly you would need to develop at least a basic set of rules in order to prevent chaos from reigning and people getting hurt. There are books written and films made about when this doesn't happen – and one thing's for sure: it isn't pretty!

In actual fact, not having any rules or laws does not lead to freedom or enjoyment, but chaos. If we are allowed to do what we want, then today's reading tells us that we become trapped and caught by our own wrongdoing. Rules protect us and help us to live our lives fully. Because we have laws and a police force to enforce those laws, we can go about our daily lives feeling secure. We are set free by the laws we have in place.

 ### *Think*

Think of some of the places where people do live in fear: perhaps a country with a corrupt police force or no clear/ fair government in power. Pray that God would help to bring about a stable and fair government and set these people free.

HOT TOPIC | DISCIPLINE 2

Everybody makes mistakes

READ: MATTHEW 18:21–35

KEY VERSE V35
'This is how my heavenly Father will treat each of you unless you forgive your brother or sister from your heart.'

Remember looking at this story a couple of weeks ago? We're going to take it at a slightly different angle this time.

Have you ever known a parent who seems to think that their children can do no wrong? Even if their children act rude or nasty, to their parents they are still little angels, perfect in every way. This is a good example of exactly why we need to have our mistakes pointed out to us and why we need to be disciplined.

Today's reading describes a man who behaved in a particularly nasty way. Despite the kindness shown to him in regard to his own debt, he refused to have mercy on someone who was in debt to him. And he was punished by being thrown into prison.

If we fail to show mercy and forgiveness towards others then we end up in a mess of anger and bitterness. God isn't cruel and doesn't 'torture' us Himself, but maybe He sometimes leaves us to the consequences of our actions to teach us – and make us more loving and forgiving. God is faithful to us, even though sometimes we are not faithful to Him. Whatever we have done wrong, He is prepared to forgive. If we have been given this grace, then we also have a responsibility to show the same grace to others.

HOT TOPIC | DISCIPLINE 2

➕ *Challenge*
Who was the last person who hurt you? Have you forgiven this person? Why not take a step to do so now?

Push through the wall

 READ: HEBREWS 12:1–13

KEY VERSE V10
'God disciplines us for our good, in order that we may share in his holiness.'

In order to achieve anything in life, we often have to endure hardship along the way. For academic success, we need to study hard. To achieve sporting success, we need to be disciplined in our training.

Today's passage reminds us that the Christian life is not always easy. Sometimes we might even feel like giving up. Marathon runners talk about 'hitting the wall' when they feel as if they can go no further. However, when they keep on pushing past this wall of exhaustion, they are somehow able to go on. Today's passage tells us that when we feel like this, we should fix our eyes on Jesus and allow ourselves to be inspired by Him.

God isn't going to simply remove all the obstacles from our path and make our lives easy. We don't become Christians in order to have an easier life. However, when we are struggling, we should be assured that God is there with us as our coach, every step of the way. Unlike an earthly coach or father, God really does always know best. We really can trust in Him and His instructions for our life.

 ## *Challenge*
Today's reading talks about throwing off the things that hold us back, such as sin. Is there anything that you think God, your coach, is calling you to throw off? Accept His discipline and instruction because He truly does know what is best for you.

HOT TOPIC | DISCIPLINE 2

The greater good

READ: ROMANS 8:28–39

KEY VERSE V39
'neither height nor depth, nor anything else in all creation, will be able to separate us from the love of God'

In Romans 8, Paul challenges us to see the big picture. As we reflected yesterday, during times of trouble it is so easy to think that God has abandoned us, and yet the Bible and history are full of stories that show how wrong that idea is.

Paul is clear that God doesn't always seem to help in the way that we expect, but that 'God causes everything to work together'. So a situation might not be what we had hoped for or expected, but God is still very much in control. He causes things to happen so that we become more like Jesus, and this is a process that He will continue to work on. The passage then goes on to highlight that suffering is not the end of the story, but is just a part of the story. God cares so much for us that He gave up Jesus. But through Jesus' suffering, God was able to work for good.

When we are in the midst of a time of discipline or trial, we need to remember that God holds the bigger picture. He knows what He is doing. There is nothing, not one single thing, that could come our way and take us away from His love. Are we prepared to put our trust in Him?

HOT TOPIC | DISCIPLINE 2

Pray

Father God, help us in the midst of trouble, pain and suffering to see Your big picture. Allow us to understand that victory is Yours and nothing in all creation will ever be able to separate us from Your love. Amen.

Watch me

≡ **READ: 2 THESSALONIANS 3:6–13**

KEY VERSE V9
'We did this… in order to offer ourselves as a model for you to imitate.'

For much of the last couple of weeks, we have looked at our response to being disciplined ourselves. But this is only one side of the story. As we get older, we are increasingly faced with taking on the role of showing others the right way to live and setting an example to younger people. Perhaps you help out with children's work at church, mentor a younger pupil at school or earn money through babysitting – or maybe you have younger brothers or sisters. Even if you can't think of a specific situation that is like one of the situations listed above, I have no doubt that some younger people, somewhere, look up to you in some way.

Today's reading gives some wise principles for all those of us involved in setting rules and setting an example to others. Are we doing it for the satisfaction of feeling powerful and exploiting people? Or are we exercising our authority in a godly way? It's important to remember that we, like others, aren't perfect – but we can still make a difference. Our motivation in leading and showing others the right way should be to serve them, help them and give them a good model of living to copy.

○ *Think*

Think about the people who might look up to you. How do you show them, teach them and help them to live godly lives of freedom? What is your motivation for doing this?

02

TALENT

Attitude problem
READ: 1 SAMUEL 15:10–29

KEY VERSE V11
'I regret that I have made Saul king, because he has turned away from me and has not carried out my instructions.'

How often do you hear about either celebrities or people you know who have 'gone off the rails'? So often in the media we encounter stories of people who are really talented and have had really promising futures, but have gone down a path that's meant it's all come crashing down. Drugs, drinking, affairs, anger – these are some of the things that have stopped really talented people doing what they do best. It's not that their talent has gone, but the way they are living is making a mess of it.

Saul had started out so promisingly. He was tall, handsome and influential; every inch a king (see 1 Sam. 9). People probably wouldn't have been surprised when God chose Saul as king of Israel. But somewhere along the line, Saul got complacent. He started thinking that he could ignore God, do what he wanted and rule Israel in the way he wanted to. Saul thought he could stop listening to God and still be king. That was the turning point. God rejected Saul as king, not because Saul wasn't talented, but because he was ignoring God. The way he was living had made a mess and it was time for someone else to take over.

Our skill and talent in themselves aren't what matter. What really matters is our attitude. As we use our talents, are we doing things God's way? Or are we getting complacent and just doing what we want? Let's learn from the example of Saul and seek to have the right attitude. It's then that God will put our talents to good use.

Pray

Ask God to help you see whether your attitude towards Him is right. If you know you haven't been obeying God in something, now would be a good time to make a fresh start. Commit to listening to God and obeying Him in everything.

Bad hair day

READ: JUDGES 16:4–22

KEY VERSE V17
'So he told her everything. "No razor has ever been used on my head"'

It's easy for our talent to go to our head, and this story is one of that happening a bit too literally. Samson had been given superhuman strength from God, but in a bizarre Old Testament twist, the degree of Samson's strength was linked to the length of his hair. Samson was told this and as he listened to God and kept his hair on, he was used by God in amazing ways. He knew that if anyone found out where his strength came from, he would be in a whole heap of trouble.

But Samson began to rely on himself, and left God out of the picture. Eventually he let his secret slip to a woman working for Israel's enemies, the Philistines. Unsurprisingly, he woke up one morning to find a colder head, a lot of sweeping up to be done, and the start of his downfall.

Samson was doing fine. His talent was being used well, until he started relying on himself and thinking he didn't need God's help. It's in these moments when we begin to think too much of ourselves that we are at our most vulnerable. For our talent to be used to its full potential we need to remember where it came from. Because if our talent goes to our heads, it could end up costing us our hair!

HOT TOPIC | TALENT 2

Pray
Ask God for humility, to keep you relying on Him, rather than getting proud and trusting your own talent to get you through.

Should you choose to accept it...

READ: JUDGES 6:11–24

KEY VERSE V15
'how can I save Israel? My clan is the weakest in Manasseh, and I am the least in my family.'

Gideon didn't think he had what it took to be a leader. This possibility was so far from what he was expecting that he kept testing God just to make sure this was actually coming from Him. He just couldn't get his head around it. You can read what happened next for yourself, but after a series of odd events he ended up leading Israel to one of their greatest military victories. He never saw it coming.

The Bible is full of people being used when they least expect it. Jonah was a reluctant prophet who saved a city, Moses had a stutter and Peter was a lowly fisherman who went on to lead the Early Church. God worked through these people (and a whole load of others) when they least expected it, unearthing talents they didn't know they had. The brilliant news is that He does the same today.

God may not be asking you to lead the Israelite army, but He has amazing plans and talents for you, perhaps where you least expect them. The question is, are you open to whatever God has for you to do? Often when we move out of where we are comfortable, we rely on God and He can use us in more exciting ways than we could possibly imagine.

Challenge

It's time to get out of your comfort zone! Ask God to lead you and to work through you in unexpected ways this week.

HOT TOPIC | TALENT 2

Get back up

READ: LUKE 9:37–43

KEY VERSE V40
'I begged your disciples to drive it out, but they could not.'

James, the inventor, had failed. He had a great idea but he just couldn't quite get it right. Every time he would change one thing, something else would go wrong. But he believed he had something worth sticking at. He learnt from each attempt and kept going. Eventually he had amassed 5,126 failed attempts. But number 5,127 was to be a success. The man's invention? A particular type of vacuum cleaner. His name? James Dyson. If it weren't for all those failures, we wouldn't have those clever bag-less machines that we have today. Failure was vital to help James learn.

In this story some disciples came back to Jesus saying that things hadn't gone how they'd expected; that they'd failed. Did Jesus cast them off as failures? No. He helped them to learn from the experience. Those disciples didn't let their failure define them. In fact, once Jesus' time on earth had come to an end it was these disciples who started the spread of the gospel across the entire world. Talent doesn't come pre-packaged for success. We will fail at times. But if we learn from this and move on, great things can still happen.

HOT TOPIC | TALENT 2

🔍 *Think*

Have you failed at something recently? What have you learnt from it? Do you shy away from situations where you might fail? Have the courage to try, fail and learn.

Give it a go

READ: LUKE 10:1–20

KEY VERSE V17
'The seventy-two returned with joy and said, "Lord, even the demons submit to us in your name."'

They say you either love or hate Marmite. That's understandable, given the unexplainable taste of it. But here's the thing: to find out if you love it, you're going to have to try it. A similar thing can be said about us using our talents. Sometimes you'll only learn if you're good at something by trying it. You just have to get stuck in.

The model Jesus uses here is fantastic. The disciples have been hanging round with Him for a while, seeing the way He operates. So when their time comes, does He ease them into the work? Oh no. He sends them out into the world, on their own. Terrifying, eh? As much as it was a risk for the disciples to try this stuff, it was equally risky for Jesus – He had a reputation to maintain! He sent His followers off with a few words of advice (about dust and wiping their feet, oddly). They learnt what they could do by doing it. They didn't get everything right (most of us don't at first), but they learnt a lot more than they would have done by just watching Jesus do it.

So go on, try something different. You'll never know if you can do it if you don't give it a go.

➕ *Challenge*

Is there something you've been thinking about doing to serve God or the people around you? Chat it through with some other Christians and make a plan.

Wise guy

READ: 1 KINGS 3:16–28

KEY VERSE V28
'When all Israel heard the verdict the king had given, they held the king in awe, because they saw that he had wisdom from God'

Last weekend, we looked at the end of Saul's rule over Israel. Saul was talented, but blew it simply by ignoring God. Two generations on, we see a turning point in Solomon's life. King Solomon wasn't like his predecessor. He relied on God to make him a good king and prayed for God's wisdom to help him lead Israel (1 Kings 3:3–14). Today, on Good Friday, we are reminded of God's brilliant wisdom in sending Jesus into the world. For a moment it looked hopeless, but His wisdom showed through three days later.

In verses 16–28, we see an example of Solomon's impressive wisdom in action. Wisdom is a fantastic talent to have. It can have a dramatic impact on the people around us, as it did for the women who came to Solomon. Solomon himself urges us to get wise, whatever else we do (Prov. 4:7).

And in the New Testament, James assures us that God's wisdom is available to any of us if we just ask (James 1:5). Because of what Jesus did on the cross, we can approach God and ask Him for wisdom, just as Solomon did. And we can be confident that we will receive it. We can then use God's wisdom to help and influence the people around us.

Pray

However wise you think you are already, ask God to give you His wisdom. Then use that wisdom to help the people around you.

HOT TOPIC | TALENT 2

Weekend

Spotted!

READ: LUKE 5:1–11

☰ KEY VERSE V10
'Jesus said to Simon, "Don't be afraid; from now on you will fish for people."'

Happy Easter!

What a brilliant day to celebrate the resurrection of our Lord Jesus, and to be reminded of the amazing impact He has on our lives – especially within the area of talents!

Sometimes a person's talents lie there, untapped, waiting to be used – kind of like an old book gathering dust on a shelf. We need to unearth those talents.

Jesus has an amazing ability to spot potential where no one else does. Just look at His disciples: the fishermen, the tax collectors, the religious nutters, the ones the rest of society had given up on – they really were quite the group. Jesus took them off the shelf and turned them into a bunch of people ready to change the face of the world. He trusted them with the good news of His triumph over sin and sent them out to let the world know. Jesus brought out the best in these people, even when no one else knew it was there. Others may have written these people off, but that didn't stop Him.

We can do the same. Make an effort to look for the talent in the people around you. Once you've found it, do everything you can to encourage these people and nurture their talents. Help them discover their talents, hone them and use them for God's kingdom. Today we're reminded of the greatest news ever – that Jesus defeated death and sin, and we can be forgiven through Him. So let's make every effort to use the brilliant talents He gives us to spread His message, and encourage others to do the same.

 ## Think

What potential can you see in the people around you? How can you invest in someone and help them discover and use their talents? And how might these talents help other people to know who Jesus is and what He has done for them?

He's the healer

READ: ACTS 9:36–43

KEY VERSE V40
'Turning towards the dead woman, he said, "Tabitha, get up." She opened her eyes, and seeing Peter she sat up.'

It's not quite accurate to call Peter's ability to heal in today's reading a 'talent'. This isn't a natural ability, but a supernatural one. (A while ago, we mentioned the difference between a talent and a spiritual gift and this is an example of that difference.)

At times, God works through an individual to heal another individual, but this actually has very little to do with the natural talents of either person. This kind of healing is nothing less than the power of God working through a human being.

Knowing that we're unable to heal anyone shouldn't be discouraging; it should be liberating and comforting. We can pray for someone who's sick, knowing that the results aren't up to us. God is the one who will take care of that. Although none of us have a natural talent for healing, God might still use us as His agents for healing others. This should inspire us to keep praying for people we know who are sick. It's risky to pray for this kind of thing. For whatever reason, God might not heal the person we're praying for. But our chances of seeing someone healed are considerably higher if we bother praying!

HOT TOPIC | TALENT 2

 Pray

Who do you know who is sick? Pray for that person and ask God to heal them. Also, listen to what God might have to say about His plans for this person.

Building up

 READ: PHILEMON 4–7

KEY VERSE V7
'Your love has given me great joy and encouragement, because you... have refreshed the hearts of the Lord's people.'

Not all talents are obvious and spectacular. People who are confident, outgoing and seem comfortable on a stage get a lot of attention, but often it's the quieter ones who make a real difference; the ones who are talented in helping and caring for other people and quietly committed to doing just that. Maybe you know some people like that.

Some talents are really impressive. If you can walk around on your hands, good for you! But don't make the mistake of thinking you have to be loud and outgoing to do anything significant. You might be talented in showing kindness to people in a way that 'refreshes their hearts'. Using that talent can make a huge difference to someone who needs encouragement and comfort – often more than we will ever know.

Even Paul, possibly the most influential church leader and teacher who ever lived, needed the encouragement that someone like Philemon could give him. There are lots of hurting people in our world right now, so if you know that encouragement is a talent you have, please use it! Keep in mind the enormous difference it can make. And if you're not sure whether you have this talent, give it a try!

HOT TOPIC | TALENT 2

 Think

How can you refresh the hearts of God's people? Whether or not you think you're talented in caring for other people, ask for God's help in this.

Inside out

READ: 1 SAMUEL 16:1–13

KEY VERSE V7
'The Lord does not look at the things people look at. People look at the outward appearance, but the Lord looks at the heart.'

It's amazing the way talent affects how we look at someone. With shows like *Britain's Got Talent*, *The Voice* and *The X Factor*, we can really easily judge someone based on their talent (or lack of it!). And there are the times when we judge someone's talent based on their appearance, only to be proved wrong.

Yes, talent is important. God has given us all different things we can do. But we must balance that with the fact that our talent doesn't make us any more valuable. The person who tries to do a magic trick on TV but spectacularly fails is just as valuable and important as Simon Cowell himself. David didn't look like anything particularly special, but God loved him, chose him and had big plans for him anyway.

God's love for us is unconditional. It does not depend on whether we can sing well on a stage in front of some cameras. Your talent doesn't define you any more than your haircut or where you went on holiday last summer. So we shouldn't judge someone else because of their talent, any more than we should because of their appearance.

➕ *Challenge*

Think about how you treat people. Is it based on what the world says about them or the way God looks at them? Choose to love and accept the people around you, regardless of their talent, just as God does.

HOT TOPIC | TALENT 2

On the way up

 READ: PROVERBS 22:17–29

KEY VERSE V29

'Do you see someone skilled in their work? They will serve before kings; they will not serve before officials of low rank.'

Have you ever discovered a band you love but no one else seems to have heard of their music? Have you then seen that band become massively famous? It can bring a strange mixture of emotions, can't it? On the one hand, there's an element of pride that you found this band before your friends did. On the other, a tinge of jealousy that they are now no longer just your thing. More than anything, though, when something like this happens, you're delighted that people so talented are getting the recognition they deserve.

Someone with talent deserves to have that talent noticed, and to have more opportunities to use it. Fortunately, most of the time, talent does get noticed – but that isn't guaranteed, and sometimes it takes a little help for this to happen. So if you see someone with obvious talent, it's great to help other people see that talent too. Don't assume that people already realise their own talents, and don't assume they realise the talents of others.

Look around you. What talents can you see in others? How can you encourage them to use that talent to honour God?

 ## Pray

Pray for particular people you know who have clear talents. Ask God to help them hone their talents and use them for His glory. And look out for opportunities to encourage each of these people.

HOT TOPIC | TALENT 2

Not the obvious choice

READ: ACTS 9:19–31

KEY VERSES VV26–27
'[Saul] tried to join the disciples, but they were all afraid of him... But Barnabas took him and brought him to the apostles.'

Today's reading is all about Saul who became Paul. This guy wrote many of the books that are in the New Testament, spread the good news about Jesus to a whole load of places, and even has churches named after him today. But he didn't start off looking very promising.

Saul had a reputation for not just disliking Christians, but having them killed! Understandably, some people didn't feel easy about letting him into their inner circle. However, Barnabas saw potential in Saul, chose to believe he had changed and took a chance on him, even though others didn't feel the same way.

God often uses the people who we least expect in order to do great things. Some of the best youth workers have grey hair, some of the best speakers start off quite shy and some of the best worship leaders have never owned a checkered shirt. We're encouraged to not write people off so easily but to stop and consider what God might be doing in and through them.

As we near the end of this series of readings, let's do all we can to become people who not only use our own talents but celebrate the talents of others, even when that isn't the easiest thing.

HOT TOPIC | TALENT 2

 Challenge
Who do you know who has a clear talent? How can you help them use and develop that talent? Look for an opportunity today.

**WEEKEND
18/19 APR**

THE TRINITY

Alpha and Omega

READ: JOB 38:1–18

KEY VERSE V4
'Where were you when I laid the earth's
foundation? Tell me, if you understand.'

The first and last letters of the Greek alphabet are
alpha α and omega Ω. Most of the New Testament
was originally written in Greek. In this last section
looking at the Holy Trinity, we're going to think
about God being the beginning and the end – that
is, being present before the beginning of time and
always being there forever into eternity.

Today's verses are brilliant for helping us to
understand our creator God; the God who made the
seas and oceans (v8), gave orders to the morning
(v12), and knows every part of the vast expanse
of the earth (v18). (Read the rest of the chapter to

see what else our amazing God created!) This Holy Trinity is the creator and sustainer of the universe and of life itself, in all its complexity and detail – from the vastness of our galaxy to the absurdity of a jellyfish. The Holy Trinity is present throughout creation. Right from the beginning, the Father, Jesus and Spirit worked in relationship at making the world, and even today we can marvel at God's fingerprints on creation.

Just putting this chapter of the Bible into context, Job was a man who didn't have an easy life, to say the least. And during the first 37 chapters of this Bible book, we see Job debating and arguing with his friends and being annoyed with God. Then comes this amazing chapter. The Lord finally has His turn to speak … and it's enough to knock your socks off! Our God is undoubtedly powerful and in control. Instead of letting life get to us, let's take our problems to God, who created all life!

Challenge

Look around outside today and take notice of God's creation. Admire it! This Holy Trinity we worship is always at work, within and throughout creation.

'In the beginning...'

READ: GENESIS 1:1–5

KEY VERSE V2
'the Spirit of God was hovering over the waters.'

Have you ever had the feeling that you have been there at the very beginning of something? Maybe a new footballer at your local club is breaking through into the first team and you just know he's going all the way to the England team. Maybe you've been to a gig and the support act is so good you know that before long they will also be huge.

Here, the Holy Spirit is present at the very dawn of time: before the creation of the world, before Jesus is born as a human thousands of years later, and before the disciples nervously wait in the upper room after Jesus' resurrection and ascension. The Spirit of God is present throughout creation, and exists inside and outside of time itself. Big stuff!

God speaks and the world is created. Have you ever wondered who He was talking to when He says, 'Let there be light' (v3)? The Trinity is a relational God. The three persons of the Trinity are talking to each other, discussing what is needed for life to exist on the planet they've made. The Spirit of God is the life force of creation which, together with the Father and the Son, upholds all things in existence.

 Pray

Thank You, Lord, that You were present – Father, Son and Holy Spirit – at the creation of the world. Thank You that You are a relational God who longs to be my friend and to draw me deeper into Your mysterious and awesome love and power. Amen.

CORE THEME | THE TRINITY 3

Heaven's kitchen

READ: JOHN 1:1–5

KEY VERSE V3
'Through him all things were made; without him nothing was made that has been made.'

We've looked so far at the Spirit's involvement in creation, but what about Jesus? John writes that the Word (Jesus) was with God and was God. It's an amazing and really helpful glimpse of the Trinity – God deciding to make everything through the Son.

Jesus gave life to everything that was created. By the Son's life, light came into the world. Jesus goes on to tell His disciples that He is 'the light of the world' (John 8:12) and interestingly Genesis tells us that on the first day of creation God said, 'Let there be light' (Gen. 1:3).

Here we see a creator God, fully involved, with sleeves rolled up and hands dirty, shaping the universe. The Savoy Grill is a very posh restaurant in London owned by Gordon Ramsay. Without the head chef's say-so, no dish is allowed out of the kitchen, because his reputation is on the line with every meal that is served. Sloppy work is certainly not tolerated. Like a perfectionist chef, nothing but perfection was going to be served up by God.

Because the Trinity is perfect, God's plan for creation was perfect: through the Son a perfect universe was created by God. Of course, we mess up sometimes but we can always talk to God about it. He is *always* loving and gracious.

❝ *Share*

'I generally think of the Trinity as individual beings working together.' (Ethan, 17)

Unfogging the future

READ: ISAIAH 53:1–6

KEY VERSE V3
'He was despised and rejected by mankind, a man of suffering, and familiar with pain.'

In the *Harry Potter* series, Sybill Trelawney is a professor at Hogwarts. She can see into the future and make prophecies; the most important one being about Lord Voldemort and how he will be vanquished by Harry.

The Old Testament has many prophecies of Jesus coming to earth as the second person of the Trinity. They were usually given to select people in the form of visions about the future – things that had not yet happened. These weren't fictional, they were God-given and real. He wanted to show the world that He is the beginning and the end.

Today we read Isaiah's prophecy, which details the events of Jesus' life and death, hundreds of years before they even came to pass. Jesus fulfils this and many other prophecies about the details of His earthly life: the town in which He is born, His escape to Egypt, His heart for the poor and sick, the type of death He suffers and, ultimately, His resurrection.

God uses Isaiah's words to affect not only his contemporaries, but also many others in future generations. We can marvel at the amazing foresight Isaiah was given and know that our God always sees what's next!

CORE THEME | THE TRINITY 3

66 *Share*

'I generally think of the Trinity as three aspects of God.'
(Cam, 15)

He is the champion

≡ **READ: REVELATION 5:1–14**

KEY VERSE V6
'Then I saw a Lamb, looking as if it had been slain, standing at the centre of the throne'

→ Unfortunately, England has not won the World Cup since 1966. It's hard and sometimes even a bit emotional for fans to watch their national football team walking off the pitch with with such disappointment on their faces. The whole nation groans as, yet again, the expectancy of winning a tournament is not realised. Maybe 2022 will be their year...

Here, in the book of Revelation, John describes to us the scene in heaven. The scrolls are about to be opened, yet there is no one found among all the people present who is worthy of this highly-esteemed task. Then the scene focuses on a lamb, looking as if it had been slaughtered. The lamb represents Jesus who was sacrificed for us – it is an image of an obedient Son and a murdered member of the Trinity. If things ended there, we would certainly have dejected faces and nothing to celebrate. However, God allowed Jesus to die in order to save humankind from its sin. And it wasn't the end of the story – celebration was coming!

The chapter ends on a high, with the whole of heaven joining together in worship for the lamb that was slain. When we remember the Trinity's amazing plan for our salvation, let's also sing and worship – God has won!

❝ *Share*

'I sometimes think of the Trinity as like the legs of a camera tripod; if one's missing, everything falls down.' (Josh, 16)

I did it His way

READ: PSALM 2:1–12

KEY VERSE V4
'The One enthroned in heaven laughs; the Lord scoffs at them.'

How many people do you think have a wrong image of God? Perhaps they see God as an old man in heaven, all dressed in white, and very distant from what's going on on planet Earth. Or maybe they see Him as a tubby 'Santa-type' God who will let sins go unpunished at the end of time because He is just gentle and kind. Or others possibly see Him as a vindictive God who reaches down from heaven with a big stick, hurting people just for the sake of His own entertainment.

According to the psalmist, God fits none of the above images but is very different altogether. The Lord Almighty, this mysterious three-in-one God, is a God who laughs at human plans that attempt to oppose His mighty purposes. He also might have a little chuckle when we make plans without involving Him. Not in a mean, Bond-villain way, more in an amused, 'My plans are better' way.

Psalm 2 teaches us that God is sovereign. He is King. The Trinity reigns! The great heavenly plan of salvation – set into motion at Jesus' birth – will one day come to completion when all who love God are gathered to be with Him forever. No ruler, no power, no politician, no authority, no army or weapon will ever stop the saving plan of the Trinity being worked out on earth – wow!

CORE THEME | THE TRINITY 3

 Share

'I sometimes think of the Trinity like a triangle, all sides being both different but the same.' (Jacob, 16)

Weekend

25/26 APR

God is...

READ: REVELATION 1:1–8

≡ KEY VERSE V8
'I am the Alpha and the Omega... who is, and who was, and who is to come'

Have you ever played Taboo? It's a game where you have to describe a word on a card without actually saying the word. It's not that easy. Imagine your card said 'God', how would you describe God? What words can adequately do justice to our awesome, Almighty God? No human could even try unless God Himself had revealed Himself to that person and then given them the words!

In the beginning of the book of Revelation, John uses time to describe God, calling Him the God who always was and who is and who is still to come. This description shouts aloud the timelessness of God. We've previously read about how He was even there before the beginning of time as we know it!

Time is a limitation that we, as humans, are constrained by: time for bed, time for school etc. We age and feel the effects of time. We sometimes feel like we just don't have enough time in the day! However, as we see from John's description, we serve a God who is not constrained by time, but instead rules over it with power.

Another similar description of God, used by John in Revelation, is that He is the Alpha and Omega – the beginning and the end. Our great and glorious God rules as the Trinity over time and space. The amazing revelation that John received is written down for us and describes God in a series of visual ways. Go back and read it again! What a mighty Trinitarian picture! He is the God of all time, the Father, Son and Holy Spirit.

 Pray

Father, thank You for Your revelation to us of Your mighty power and awesome might. Thank You that You are the God of space and time, that You even broke into time as God the Son and raised Him from the dead by the power of God the Spirit. Amen.

Justice

≡ **READ: REVELATION 20:11–15**

KEY VERSE V12
'The dead were judged according to what they had done as recorded in the books.'

Today we focus in on the Father, whose role for the end of time is to judge all. The Father sits on the throne to judge fairly all the injustice that has ever taken place in the world – all the pain and sorrow, war and suffering that has been caused to humanity by humanity. Even death itself is finally judged and punished.

The great master plan of the Trinity, shown throughout the Bible, now ends with this scene. Jesus has beaten death and sin. The enemy of the Church, Satan, is defeated and the Church has, through the power of the Spirit, increased through the centuries, bringing many people to believe the truth of the gospel message. Finally, the Father has His say.

The image of hell is not a popular one in today's churches but Jesus spoke a lot about hell in the Bible. However, as people with a living, breathing friendship with the Holy Trinity, it's important for us to remember that we have nothing to fear in this life or the next, for we have been won forever through the saving work of the Father, Son and Holy Spirit.

❝ *Share*

'I once felt a "nudge" from the Holy Spirit to pray for healing for my friend. My friend has already been partly healed.'
(Daniel, 15)

Can you repeat that please?

READ: ISAIAH 6:1–8

KEY VERSE V3
'Holy, holy, holy is the LORD Almighty; the whole earth is full of his glory.'

Why do we use repetition? It's everywhere! In TV programmes like *Location, Location, Location*; songs like 'Money, Money, Money'; or important announcements like 'Brace! Brace! Brace!' Is it just to show its importance or to drum into us a particular kind of message?

Isaiah is given this wonderful vision of heaven, with the Lord seated on a throne and the angels surrounding Him. All of heaven shouts, 'Holy, holy, holy'. Is the word 'Holy' repeated because God is so holy and as humans we need to understand this, or is it repeated because God is, in fact, three in one – the mystery that is the Trinity?

The one place where we will understand the Trinity more easily will be in heaven. We will be in perfect relationship with God and we'll see, sense and know our three-in-one God for ourselves. Can you imagine the scene in heaven: God seated on the throne, the angels singing, and YOU there too? As Christians on earth now, we are caught up in the mystery of the Trinity; in heaven we will be amazed at the majesty of the Trinity. All seeds of doubt will vanish when we are faced with the sovereignty and glory of God.

Share

'I have not felt a "nudge" from the Holy Spirit to do anything yet, but I hope that it will happen one day.' (Grace, 14)

CORE THEME | THE TRINITY 3

One day...

≡ READ: PHILIPPIANS 2:5–11

KEY VERSE V10
*'that at the name of Jesus every knee should bow,
in heaven and on earth and under the earth'*

What sort of things do you tend to look forward to? Maybe the summer holidays or a nice birthday treat? Perhaps a film that's due to be released soon, or an important match that the team you support are playing? We all look forward to things in our lives and long for these moments to come.

In the same way, God looks forward to the day when we will be with Him in heaven forever and the great Trinitarian plan to rescue the human race is finally fulfilled. In writing to the Philippians, Paul tells us that 'at the name of Jesus every knee should bow'. When we are faced with this glorious God and go to be with Him forever, we will be brought to our knees in wonder, awe and joy.

This scene will be better than any church service, celebration, worship conference or festival we go to – it will be worship on a scale like no other. We will see God in all His glory and this will cause us to sing and praise Him, surrounded by angels and fellow believers. We will be caught up in perfect worship of our amazing God.

❝ *Share*

'I was at my church's youth club when I felt a prompt from the Holy Spirit to pray for someone's neck. We prayed and they were healed.' (Ethan, 17)

CORE THEME | THE TRINITY 3

Nothing compares to You

READ: PSALM 86:1–10

KEY VERSE V8
'Among the gods there is none like you, Lord; no deeds can compare with yours.'

We've come to the end of this issue of *Mettle* and our look at the Trinity! Today let's conclude what we've learnt about our three-in-one God by briefly looking at how gods of other world religions compare with Him. How different is our Trinitarian God to the god of the Muslims or the many gods of the Hindus, or the Buddhists?

The psalmist declares that our God is completely different from all world religions, faiths and values. He calls on the Lord to hear him and answer him. This is a God who is interested in his life; a relational God who is kind and forgiving.

In Buddhism, we see a human religious philosophy; in Hinduism, a religion that worships thousands of gods. In Islam and Judaism we learn of two religions that worship only one God, not the Trinitarian God of Christianity.

We worship a God who respects our choice and offers His friendship and forgiveness freely. He is a God who understands everything we experience because He made it all and walked the earth Himself as a man.

We hope that this study on the Trinity has given you a hunger to go deeper in your understanding of this awesome God we worship and become closer to Him, day by day.

 Challenge

Write down some key points you've learnt during this study of the Trinity. If there are any questions you are still unsure of, why not talk to a leader at church.